# Stretched But Not Broken

*The Portrait of a Missionary*

## Lois P. Miller

All profits from *Stretched But Not Broken* go to encourage the Evangelical Church in Spain and Ecuador by means of adding to Education Scholarship funds and ministry to national Seminarians and Pastors.

For more information regarding the Miller family, present missionary projects, or reproduction of this publishing

Contact:  Bill and Darlene MIller
          c/o NMSI
          P.O. Box 547
          Fort Myers, FL 33902

For more information about the ministry of OMS International
Contact:  OMS International, Inc.
          P.O. Box A
          Greenwood, IN 46142

# Stretched But Not Broken

*The Portrait of a Missionary*

Lois P. Miller

Faithful Life Publishers
North Fort Myers, FL

www.FLPublishers.com

*Stretch But Not Broken*

Copyright © 2000, revised edition 2009

All rights reserved by William and Darlene Miller

ISBN: 978-0-9821408-1-9

Prepared by: Darlene Miller

Published by: Faithful Life Publishers
North Fort Myers, FL  33903

www.FLPublishers.com

Scripture quotations from the King James Version

All rights reserved. No part of this publication may be reproduced, stored in a retrieval system, or transmitted in any form or by any means—electronic, mechanical. photocopy, recording, or any other—except for brief quotations in printed reviews, without the prior permission of Faithful Life Publishers and/or William Miller or Darlene Miller.

Printed in the United States of America
18  17  16  15  14  13  12  11  10  09     2 3 4 5 6

# DEDICATED
*to my brothers and sisters:*

*Charlotte Ann Francescangeli*

*Ronald Lee Pankuch*

*Nancy Joan Kime*

*Barbara Lynn Wickwire*

*John Pankuch, Jr.*

*and*

*Beverly Sue Holt*

*And to my beloved husband,*

*William George Miller Jr.*

*and our son*

*William George Miller III*

# FOREWORD

My wife, Lois, is a good steward of her time and her talents. I look at her, occupied with the things of the Lord, and I thank my God for her.

As she was sharing the incidents of this book with me, I would naturally think of related happenings. Sometimes I made suggestions. Often she would answer, "I can't put EVERYTHING in this book!"

So as you read the following pages you may wish to know more about a certain year or a specific responsibility. I wish she would have shared more about our deputation ministry experiences, especially in the British Isles—but "she can't put everything in this book."

So I made the suggestion that she start another book. After all, she is retired now although she prefers to call it "retreaded" because she is in no way inactive.

I am grateful to the Lord for all the richness of spirituality and emotional awareness that Lois has brought to my life. May you be blessed and grateful, too, as you read the following pages.

*Bill Miller*

# INTRODUCTION

What was my purpose in writing this book, you may ask. First of all, my heart was very full. I felt constrained to write some of the memories stored in my journals, letters, and diaries. Secondly, many of our supporters, prayer partners, and friends of all these past years expressed their feeling that our "memoirs" would not only be entertaining, but would aid people to understand more about career missionary people.

Thirdly, anything written about REAL LIFE enhances our perspective, increases our knowledge, and gives us motivation for, shall I call it, "adventure?"

This is not a thorough autobiography. It is not a book of missionary philosophy. Mostly, it is a book of INCIDENTS INVOLVING PEOPLE…happenings that give evidence of God's sovereign control and sweet mercy. There are more episodes included from the years I was using a journal more consistently since it is easier to glean from the written notes than from my sometimes "skimpy" memory.

I have not been able to include every person with whom Bill and I have had a significant relationship. That would be impossible.

This narrative is deliberately designed so it can be read in "spurts"…so just enjoy a short "read" of one or two episodes. It will be like us meeting over a cup of tea!

I would be grateful to God if by reading this book, you are motivated to pray more consistently and informatively for the missionaries you love and support.

# TABLE OF CONTENTS

Dedication ................................................................. v
Foreward ................................................................. vi
Introduction ............................................................ vii

1. Our Call ........................................................... 17
2. Her Dream Came True ................................. 20
3. Grandma Wickwire ........................................ 24
4. Junior ............................................................... 27
5. My Grade School Christmases ..................... 31
6. A Mother's Sacrifice ..................................... 32
7. My Lying Tongue ........................................... 34
8. Junior Wasn't Perfect .................................... 35
9. For God So Loved Lois ................................. 37
10. My First Vocal Solo ....................................... 39
11. Occasions for Singing ................................... 41
12. I Knew I'd Never Marry ................................ 42
13. Our First Years Together .............................. 48
14. No More Migraines ....................................... 51
15. Disappointed .................................................. 53
16. Lessons from "Thorns" ................................. 57
17. God Cares for Jalopies .................................. 60
18. Why Doesn't He Answer the Door? ........... 62

## Ecuador

19. Language Hurdles ..................................................... 65
20. The Auca Incident ................................................... 68
21. Six Pails and Ten Dishpans Later ........................... 71
22. I Got Rid of the Garbage ......................................... 72
23. Don't Cry, Let's Pray ................................................ 76
24. I Learned from Geneva ........................................... 77
25. Battle-Scarred ........................................................... 78
26. The Factory of Gospel Choruses ........................... 79
27. "Streams" Touched Dry Lives ................................ 81
28. Bill—In a Jail Cell? .................................................. 84
29. Blessed Are the Flexible .......................................... 86
30. God Intervened ........................................................ 88
31. A Dance In the Street .............................................. 93
32. Miguel Said, "I Beat My Back Until It Bled" ...... 93
33. What Happened to the Candlestick? ................... 96
34. A Victim of the Miners .......................................... 98
35. I Could Sing ............................................................ 100
36. You Never Know Who's Watching ..................... 102
37. We Searched for Treasures in the Darkness ...... 104
38. David's Special Visitor .......................................... 109
39. Lassie Came Home! ............................................... 111
40. Billy's Pastor-Partner ............................................. 113
41. God Protects ........................................................... 115
42. God Alerted His Angels ........................................ 117
43. They Wanted a Catastrophic Take-Over ............ 119

| | |
|---|---|
| 44. Shared Victories | 121 |
| 45. "Cast Your Bread Upon the Waters…" | 123 |
| 46. Hail, Hail…the Gang's All Here! | 126 |
| 47. "Little Loco" | 128 |
| 48. It Was Unbelievable! | 131 |
| 49. Let's Test My Flexibility…Again! | 133 |
| 50. Who is My Neighbor? | 135 |
| 51. A Lesson in Perseverance | 138 |
| 52. Sight Comes to Antonio | 140 |
| 53. The Tormentor Was Forgiven | 142 |
| 54. God Held Back the Dark Clouds | 145 |
| 55. Persecution | 148 |
| 56. Blessed Are They Who Are Flexible | 150 |

## Spain

| | |
|---|---|
| 57. Our Initiation to Madrid | 153 |
| 58. Our First Friendly Neighbor | 157 |
| 59. The Chaplain Changed His Mind | 159 |
| 60. It Was Right to Write | 161 |
| 61. My Cheeks Ached From Smiling | 163 |
| 62. Astronaut Irwin Shared His Faith in Spain | 164 |
| 63. Niche #107 | 165 |
| 64. Every Hurdle Conquered | 170 |
| 65. The Girl in the Velvet Opera Cape | 173 |
| 66. A Poetess Responds | 176 |
| 67. The Evangelical Spanish Women's Union | 178 |

68. At the Sound of the Siren, Pray! ................................................. 181
69. To Look Beyond the Exterior Facade ........................................ 183
70. Single-Minded Obedience ............................................................ 186
71. Gloomy Day Calls ........................................................................... 188
72. I Was the Only Woman ................................................................. 189
73. My Darling's Accident ................................................................... 191
74. Two and a Half Years of Witness and Friendship .................... 193
75. Coffee With Friends ....................................................................... 195
76. A Test of Love .................................................................................. 198
77. Late Night Visitors ......................................................................... 200
78. The Gypsy Beggar Girl .................................................................. 202
79. Jose Was Changed ........................................................................... 204
80. Flexibility: Pliable Under Changing Conditions ..................... 206
81. My Motril Pals ................................................................................. 208
82. A Caterpillar Opened the Way ..................................................... 209
83. You're Angels Sent From God ...................................................... 212
84. With a Towel and Warm Water ................................................... 215
85. "Lois, Meet Juan" ............................................................................ 217
86. I Tearfully Returned to Madrid ................................................... 219
87. My Times Are in God's Hands ..................................................... 221
88. The Wrong Kind of Shock Absorbers ......................................... 223
89. A Step Into the Unknown ............................................................. 225

## Greece

90. She Thought I was Kidding! ..................................................228
91. Hope for Tomorrow ............................................................229
92. The Song From a Marble Slab ..............................................231
93. A Diary of Disaster ..............................................................233
94. I Had to Sing! ......................................................................238
95. The Fire Proved We Were a Good Team ..............................240
96. She Turned Her Back on God ..............................................243

## Retirement to Florida

97. I Always Send Bill Off With a Prayer and a Kiss ..................246
98. "I Hate You, I Hate You!" ....................................................248
99. A Murderer Slept in Our Guest Room ................................250
100. She Stole Away to Jesus ......................................................254

Epilogue .......................................................................................257
    by Darlene Miller

A Postscript From a Grateful Son .................................................261

## "WITH THE DRAWING OF THIS LOVE AND THE VOICE OF THIS CALLING"

by *Jennifer L. Woodruff*

*Not only what we thought we could afford,*
*Not only what we have the strength to give*
*Is asked of us; the grace that makes us live*
*Calls for a death, and all we are is poured*

*Onto an altar we did not design*
*And yet which holds us in his perfect will.*
*And in both flames and darkness keeps us still*
*And is the strength, the pillar, and the sign*

*Of all that never fails, though we are weak,*
*Of him who calls, and asks us to embrace*
*Our weakness, and our cross, to see his face---*
*And, made most strong in weakness, he will speak*

*Title is from The Cloud of Unknowing, ed. James Walsh, S.J.; Mahwah, NJ: Paulist Press, 1988 (Used by permission of the author.)

# 1 OUR CALL (1954)

Bill had good reason to be secretive! He wanted me to be as sure of God's directive as he was. While attending the missionary meetings at Cleveland Bible College in April where Dr. Dwight Ferguson spoke about evangelism in the Orient, Bill received a clear impression from the Holy Spirit. He went to the altar to confirm his heart's decision. He made himself available to God for foreign missionary service. But he didn't say a word to me about it!

I worked part-time, cared for our five-month-old son, and typed Bill's class assignments and thesis. (I have always spoiled him!) Upon graduation he received a scholarship for graduate studies at Winona Lake Summer School of Theology. He still told me nothing of his missionary call.

I'll always hold in my memory Mom standing on her porch when we stopped to say good-bye. She looked at the little Dodge, packed to capacity, and then to our smiling baby. She hugged me hard and said, "I feel that this trip is going to result in some big changes for you two. I'll always pray for your protection and guidance."

Once in a rare while there at Winona Lake, Indiana, Bill took a few minutes away from study to walk with his family around the lake. He still never said a word about missionary service. He didn't even refer to it in his prayers with me.

Meanwhile I kept busy with opportunities to use my musical talent for the Lord. One week I sang every day on the Moody radio program, "Morning Melodies," accompanied by pianist Rudy Atwood. Another week I was privileged to sing for the Pilgrim Holiness conference and the next week for the Youth for Christ meetings. Then, one morning as I walked down the main street pushing baby Billy's stroller, Chuck Ashton (who had been at Cleveland Bible College with Bill) and Bill Gillam (missionary with The Oriental Missionary Society) approached me. Bill Gillam said, "Lois, we'd like you to sing in the OMS meeting tomorrow night in the Tabernacle."

That night I sang. After the second song Dr. Ferguson (yes, the same Dr. Ferguson of the previous April!) spoke briefly then showed his movie. "Souls in Transit," portraying the plight of people without the assurance of salvation. It gripped my emotions. I began to pray, not fully comprehending the probing, then convicting, then persuading voice of the Holy Spirit. At the close of the meeting I stumbled out of the Tabernacle. Tears blurred my vision.

At home Billy was asleep in his crib. Bill sat at the kitchen table, surrounded by open books with no inclination to talk. I sat on the edge of our bed, I paced the floor, I knelt beside the bed and poured out my confusion: "God, how can I go to the foreign field as a missionary? My husband is a pastor! What's happening? My heart is persuaded that You want us on the foreign field. Oh, Lord, straighten out this mess!"

At last I fell asleep before Bill came to bed about four a.m.

The following morning Bill and I went to the restaurant to keep his appointment with Dr. Ferguson. I took my notebook to serve as secretary while Bill interviewed the evangelist, obtaining information for his thesis.

Dr. Ferguson's wife, Stella, sat beside me in the booth smiling silently. As I closed my notebook and stood to leave, Stella turned to me and asked, "Lois, what are you going to do about God's call on your life?"

I mumbled something and we left. "How did she know?" I asked myself.

Bill and I walked down the street toward our apartment. He took my hand (like he always does) but I jerked it away. In my emotional turmoil I couldn't cope with the frustration. I even was thinking, it couldn't be possible, could it?...that I was more spiritual than Bill to discern God's guidance for us!

Finally I stopped and blurted out, "Honey, what are we going to do? I think God is calling me to the mission field!"

Bill gave me his sweet, crooked smile and exclaimed, "Well, at last… thank the Lord…I've been waiting for this!"

He hugged me right there, and then we walked slowly toward home. Bill explained that, back in April he had responded "yes" to God's call for overseas service and said, "Lord, talk to my wife about this." And God did!

Both of us were convincingly drawn to OMS because of its philosophy of evangelism, church planting, and training. Within two hours the applications were in our hands. Bill Gillam himself, one of the vice-presidents, delivered them to us. That was the first week of July.

At the end of August, (after Bill's period of study) we returned to Cleveland and waited, although not very patiently. We stayed with Dad and Mother Miller, wondering about our next step. On September third I opened Dad's front door to the postman who handed me the special delivery letter from the mission. After reading the first paragraph I hollered out, "We've been accepted. We're going to South America!"

As Bill and I studied the information with the packet of offering envelopes, brochures, and meeting report forms, we rather naively turned over all the future deputation ministry to the Lord. We asked no questions about retirement plans, medical allowances, or death benefits. We were on our way!

By the third week of April 1955, (one year from the day of Bill's altar response) we boarded the plane for San Jose, Costa Rica to study Spanish. God had honored our faith. All share support was registered in the OMS Los Angeles office. We went without a commissioning service, without a personal interview with any VIP of the organization, without any psychological examination---but WITH A FAITH-FILLED PERSUASION THAT WE WERE IN GOD'S WILL. Hallelujah!

Thus began our missionary career. Thus God continued painting on the canvas of our lives with His brush of mercy and faithfulness. He has not only been faithful to us but to those whose lives preceded us. Let's go back in history to see how He had begun years before in the lives of our own family line.

# 2  HER DREAM CAME TRUE (1916)

GOD'S TIMING IS NEVER WRONG,

NEVER TOO FAST NOR TOO SLOW…

…NOTHING CAN COME AND NOTHING CAN GO

TOO SOON OR TOO LATE IN OUR DAY."

(Annie Johnson Flint)

"Dreamer…dreamer! You're not going to get your hair braided in time if you sit there gazing in the mirror all morning long!" Alice was chiding her sister, Lillian.

Her sister put down her hairbrush and sighed, "Oh, but Alice, I would so like to have a boyfriend and be making plans to marry. He's got to be kind though, and courteous, and yes, I think, elegant, too."

"Huh, none of the bachelors in your office can be called elegant! They slurp their soup and rarely open a door for a lady. Where will you ever find your dream man?"

"Who knows? But I can keep on dreaming!"

The two sisters, Alice (nineteen years old) and Lillian (just twenty-one years old) donned their felt hats before they went off to the downtown mission to sing. They sang well, but during the second song Lillian was uncomfortably aware of the stares of a very young fellow in the second row, wedged between his austere-looking parents. At the close of the meeting that very same young man approached her with a shy smile.

"Pardon me, miss, what is your name?"

"I'm Lillian Youngberg, and you?"

"William Miller. My parents are back there waiting for me, but I must tell you something very, very important."

"What's that?"

"While you were singing I was praying. It seemed to me that God whispered to my heart, 'That girl will be your wife.' And so I have to tell you, dear lady, that I'll look for you when I'm of age. I sincerely believe that one day in the future you'll be my wife."

"But, how old are you now? I'm already a grown woman and you are, well, how old ARE you?"

"Miss Youngberg, I am fifteen years old, but mature for my age. I have been studying the violin. I've completed my high school course and soon my father and I will go to the Bible Institute together to study. Please wait for me."

"Well, I can't imagine such a thing. But we'll see, we'll see."

Lillian felt silly when she told Alice about that dialogue.

---

"Come on, Lilli, we've got to leave. The Christmas service won't wait for us."

" I have to practice this piano solo just one more time. I want it to be perfect."

"Hey, maybe your William will be there! He's a musician."

"Alice, please don't make fun of him. He was very sincere, you know, and sweet and courteous. Besides, that was five years ago, and here I am, still not married, waiting for my dream man. Maybe God does want me to wait for William."

"Oh, don't be silly, sis."

---

"Alice, you'll never believe this. Sit down or you'll faint." Lillian rushed into their bedroom, flushed and excited.

"Well, well, what is it now? Have you seen your dream man? Is he elegant? Is he kind and courteous? Tell me, I'm all ears."

"I stopped at the drugstore to get some bobby pins. I had rushed out of the office and didn't bother to look in the mirror. I must have looked a sight. And there, standing inside the store was this very nice-looking man, simply but elegantly dressed. He opened the door for me, tipped his hat and said, 'Good afternoon, ma'am, with such finesse I almost swooned. Oh, Alice, I couldn't help but smile at him. Probably that was too forward of me. After all, we weren't properly introduced!"

"Hah-ah, hah-ah, maybe little Lilli has found her dream man. What color are his eyes? You know you've always been partial to blue eyes."

"Um-mmm, his eyes are deep blue with little crinkles in the corners. And his lips are full and deep pink. Oh, he's nice, Alice…so nice!"

"You saw all that in the moment he opened the door?"

"Well, I've been dreaming about him for almost six years. Yet, never once have I found a man interested in me who didn't slurp his soup… never one to hold my coat…never one to make me feel like a lady. But THIS one…oh, if I only knew who he is."

"And then? Then what would you do? You couldn't approach him and ask him to walk in the park. We're not that brazen."

"Oh, I know that. But God's timing is perfect. You know the preacher's wife is always telling us to wait for the right man."

"Sweet sister, you've been waiting…that's for sure. People talk about us, you know. We're *those spinsters*. Your responsibility as a deaconess doesn't give you many chances for meeting young men.

---

"Pardon me, Miss Youngberg, I saw you in the drugstore last week. Perhaps you don't remember me."

"How do you know my name?" Lillian was perplexed.

"Oh, don't you know me? I'm William Miller, I've been preparing myself to be your husband. Six years ago, in this very mission, I declared my intention to marry you. Don't you recall that day?"

Lillian blushed and looked down into her fur muff. "Oh, Mr. Miller, I never thought you'd come back."

"Well, I'm here now. I'm educated and ready to take a bride. I'd like to go and talk to your mother tomorrow evening if I may."

---

"How can this be, Alice? How can I feel so giddy? I hardly know the man and he's coming to see Mother tonight!"

"You're always going on and on about that dream man of yours. Maybe he's finally arrived. Oh, by the way, does he ride a white horse?" Alice chuckled.

"Don't make fun, Alice. He's real. He's kind. He's a Christian. Oh, he's a dream. He really is."

---

Even though William's mother objected to his marrying "beneath" him, the plans went forward. On a breezy day in April Lillian Olivia Youngberg and William George Miller exchanged their vows. Some people murmured, "Did you ever hear of such a thing? The bride is quite a bit older than the groom!"

And others commented, "Isn't it romantic? She actually waited for him to grow up."

The pastor declared them husband and wife. William lifted Lillian's little inexpensive veil and kissed his bride—for the very first time.

Lillian and William began their family immediately. Beautiful red-haired Ruth was their first child and Bill (William George Miller, Jr.), their first son who later became MY HUSBAND, came next.

# 3 GRANDMA WICKWIRE (1931)

Some people find satisfaction, even a sense of self-worth, in talking about their forefathers. Libraries dedicate sections to genealogies and data about tracing one's lineage. Like everyone else, Bill and I have ancestors, of course! God can trace our line all the way back to Adam. But we can't! Neither one of us has a wealth of information about our previous generations—just bits and pieces here and there.

I know nothing about my birth father. I have a sort of fantasy about him, though—that he was from some country of the Mediterranean or Aegean Seas. When Bill and I arrived in Spain there was just a bit of a problem with the different vocabulary from that of Ecuador; but otherwise, I quickly felt at ease. Often the Spaniards themselves thought I had some Spanish blood! When we arrived in Greece I had the same "at ease" feeling. In fact, I looked Greek! A couple of times I thought I saw my twin walking toward me on an Athens street.

The other day my sister Barbara and I were talking in her art gallery in Hendersonville, North Carolina. She asked, "Lois, what do you remember about Mom's mother? You knew her, didn't you? Did she pronounce her name 'Eh-va' (Eva) or 'Ee-va'?"

"Oh, she was Eva (Eh-va). I have three memories, but I can't put dates on them. The first was in her kitchen. Mom said she was a very good cook."

Bill interrupted, "Then her granddaughters followed in her footsteps!"

"That's right," Barbara answered. "What were you doing in her kitchen? Where was it?"

"In Medina, Ohio, near the railroad tracks. I remember a tall, lanky, rather large-nosed black man holding me on his knee and giving me bites from his cherry pie. Grandma was at the sink, singing in her rich contralto voice, *In the Sweet Bye and Bye*. Another black man (not as dark as my *pie-feeder*) joined in with vibrant harmony. He had a very big mouth! When I mentioned this to Aunt Undine years later she smiled and said, "The Cleveland Colored Quintet. They sang in the Medina Baptist Church and visited our Mom— because she went to that church and also made great pies." That was probably in 1931.

"Now I know where you got your singing voice from, Lois."

"Uhmm-mmm. But not just me. All of you have good voices as well. Almost all of Mom's seven kids harmonize well, as you know. Remember that Nancy sang in the Asbury College trio."

"Yes. Now tell me about more memories."

"I remember having big blond curls to my shoulders that Aunt Eva made with a comb and brush while my hair was still wet after batheing. I also remember being deliberately naughty with cousin Margaret. I don't know how she was punished, but I suppose since I was the instigator of the deed I received Grandma's wrath on my backside with her pig-bristle hairbrush. Then she put me upstairs in the attic without any supper. And know what? It was macaroni and cheese—my very, very favorite dish in those days. But I don't remember feeling angry or resentful—not even repentant!"

Bill leaned over me with a smile, "I can't believe you didn't say you were sorry."

"I don't remember that part. The other memory that I really don't like is when Grandma died. Charlotte was with me then, I think. We were out on the side lawn, sitting on the swings. Aunt Undine stood on the porch, crying and loudly blowing her nose. Mom came out and they stood with their arms around each other. Then somebody whisked us off down the street. I have a memory of asking, 'What's happening to Grandma?' She had died, but no one explained anything to us, as I remember. A couple of days later everyone was dressing up and cousin Margaret (Aunt Bonita's oldest girl), Charlotte, and I watched from the neighbor's house as they all went away in a big black car. I remember I was sitting on the swing under the big oak tree."

Barbara said, "I guess in those days tragedies like that were hushed up to protect the children. You must have been very young."

"Oh, yes—pre-schoolers."

# 4 JUNIOR (1927–1935)

"Hey, preacher, somebody left a baby on a pew in the church! And he's hollering his head off. What should I do?" The custodian was visibly confused!

"Mother, where's baby Billy? Do you have him in the kitchen!" Pastor Miller always left the children to their mother's attention after church on Sunday morning.

"Oh-oh, I got so busy trying to extricate myself from the clutches of complaining Auntie Myrtle that I rushed home without the baby. Poor thing. Poor baby!" Mother Miller hurried over to the church next door, soothed the indignant infant, and put him where he belonged.

That was Bill Miller's first introduction to the church. And one could say that ever since that day he has practically been the last person out of the church building every Sunday!

A Methodist parsonage was an ideal place to be taught about the work of the Kingdom of God, to observe both the good and the disappointing experiences of service to the Lord. To be exposed to the unique privilege of serving people for Jesus' sake. It was also a place of some deprivation and sacrifice. When the depression affected so many lives and laymen had very little to share with the struggling young pastor, there didn't seem to be enough food to feed the three Miller children. Ruth (the firstborn) and Bill (then called "Junior") had been followed by the arrival of Alice Ann. God provided a solution. Junior went to live with Grandfather and Grandmother Miller in Cleveland, Ohio for a year when he was six years old.

Grandmother Ann Patton Miller had been brought up in a well-to-do lifestyle. She loved to pray, to bring believers to the house for prayer and encouragement, to dress beautifully and appropriately, and to attend many church meetings each week. She didn't like to dirty her hands with housework. Grandfather did most of the cooking and worked as a baker. Grandfather's painstaking creativity in the bakery shop resulted in his winning a special award one year for the wedding cake he decorated that was taken to a celebration in France.

Because of Grandfather's early schedule, the family's devotional pattern was different from that of most homes. Grandfather (William Joseph Miller) went to the kitchen table to pray and read his Bible at 4:30 a.m. He very diligently maintained a dedicated obedience to God's Word. After about an hour Grandmother came from the bedroom with her Bible to join him for prayer. When little Junior came to live with them for that special year Grandmother always aroused him from slumber very early too. Junior had to join them in the kitchen. Most of the time he was cooperative although there were moments at the table when his head nodded and his eyelids drooped. Grandmother's handy hatpin, sharp and long, would prick him to attention! Although back at the parsonage the family always had devotions together, Junior remembers more vividly the devotional times with his grandparents.

Junior was almost seven years old. He had heard the Gospel all his life. Bible verses were already part of his spiritual memory. He had begun to sing hymns with his mother and sister when he was four years old, taking the alto part, even on the radio programs. He was very well acquainted with the Bible stories. As is often the case, there came a time when the moment of decision presented a crisis. The grandparents usually attended three or four church meetings each Sunday with little Junior seated between them. Again, Grandmother's threatening hatpin supplied the impetus to keep alert!

One particular Sunday night, in the Christian and Missionary Alliance Church, the message based on Psalm 139 burned into the boy's heart. When the preacher gave the invitation to go to the altar and accept the Lord Jesus as Savior, Junior squeezed out from his place between his two guardians and made his way to the front. Later, at home, Grandfather wanted to be sure that Junior understood what had happened in the church. He put the boy on a chair in front of him, opened the Bible to Psalm 51 and started to read through it with Junior. When they got to verse ten, Junior blurted out, "That's what God did for me. He did what I asked Him to do." The psalmist's prayer was "Create in me a clean heart, oh God, and renew a right spirit within me."

After his conversion experience Junior returned to Youngstown where his father pastored the Grace Methodist Church. Junior's sisters chuckled at the boy's change of attitude because of his new experience in the Lord. Always before, the three children had bickered about who would wash the dishes, who would dry, and who would escape the task. But now Junior spoke up and declared, "I'll wash and dry because Jesus doesn't want us to fight." For a while the sisters let him do it all!

That Christmas provided an experience that Bill would never forget. They didn't have abundant presents or a sumptuous feast, but God gave them an unparalleled memory.

Dad and Mother Miller took the three children to downtown Youngstown to enjoy the holiday decorations. They stopped on the street corner to listen to the Salvation Army Band. They had to leave just when the Major stepped forward to preach. Upon arriving home the children wanted to pray for the people listening to the preaching of the Gospel on the downtown street. Junior prayed, "Please, God, save somebody who really needs help."

Much later that night there was a heavy knock at the door. Dad stumbled down the stairs and turned on the porch light. A man with a stubble beard wearing wrinkled, spotted clothing smiled hesitantly at the preacher, and said, "Sir, may I come in and tell you something very important?"

He sat down, tearfully looked at Dad Miller and said, "A couple of weeks ago I came into this house and stole the clock from your mantel. I didn't use the money to give food to my kiddies. Instead, like always, I joined my buddies and got drunk. Earlier tonight I was stumbling around downtown, wondering where I could find a bottle. I stopped to listen to the Salvation Army Band and then stayed to hear the preacher. God gripped my soul. I knew I was in great need so I talked with the preacher. He explained what I needed, or rather, WHO I needed. I confessed my sin, and told God that I want to be changed. I'm so weak. I can't live like God wants me to live unless He takes over. I accepted Christ as my Lord and Savior. Now the first thing I need to do is to ask your forgiveness for stealing the clock. I want to ask how I can restore it, but I need a job. When I find one, I'll be glad to pay a little bit each week for that clock."

Dad Miller, compassionate and gentle as always, put his arms around the man as he prayed with him. Then he took some of the little money he had for Christmas and gave it to the man. "Come back tomorrow. We'll see about a job for you."

The following week (the day after Christmas) that man returned with his family. He gave testimony about God's provision. He said, "This is the very first Christmas that I've been sober. It is the first holiday that my children have had their Daddy with them at the table with good food on their plates and a little gift for each child."

Bill often refers to that experience, recognizing that God's answer to a child's sincere prayer to a loving Heavenly Father, had resulted in a man's transformation.

# 5 MY GRADE SCHOOL CHRISTMASES (1934)

Mom was always very creative, making something beautiful out of little nothings. During some of my elementary school years we lived in Cleveland, in a house that had a large double door closing off the "parlor," which today we'd call the living room. Mom, my sister Charlotte, and I made colorful paper chains. We decorated the windows with snowflakes which we cut out of white tissue paper. We marked the days off the calendar in the kitchen while enjoying the overpowering fragrances of the Slovakian filled cookies. Mom made so-o-o many of them! We thought we'd never eat them all.

But we had no Christmas tree during those preparation days. On Christmas Eve, after our supper of oyster stew and sausages, my sister and I willingly submitted to baths and bedtime. We knew the schedule. Even before we were sound asleep we'd hear scuffling and low murmuring. The pine tree was brought in and put in the parlor. Behind those closed doors a magical transformation took place. The ordinary room became the anteroom to paradise! Mom, always artistically meticulous, decorated the tree and the mantel.

The next morning we scrambled out of our bed, fussing and coaxing. Mom and Dad had to open the double doors. Then—"Oh…Ah…Oh…Ah!" The tree lights twinkled. Our eyes did, too. Christmas was real!

# 6 A MOTHER'S SACRIFICE (1936)

My Mom was a stickler for good spelling, which fascinated me. When I was in the first three grades of school she would stand at the ironing board and listen to me spell. To challenge me she grabbed the dictionary and gave me words that were not on my spelling list. This way I learned new words, too, and didn't have time to get into mischief.

I wasn't Miss Martin's pet in the third grade class, but because I was captivated by words and spelling she encouraged me to enter the school Spelling Bee. I won! Then I went to the city Spelling Bee, spurred on by Mom's coaching. But when I won in my division Mom sat with a puzzled frown on her pretty face. Miss Martin had said in glowing terms, "Lois will go to the state finals with me next Thursday. Dress her up real pretty."

I only owned a couple of skirts and plain blouses. No pretty dress with frills or pleats hung in my closet. I went to bed very early Wednesday evening, trying hard not to be nervous about the next day's challenge. We would have to leave very early.

Charlotte, my sister, just grunted and turned over when I jumped out of bed the next morning with a subdued holler. I took out my underclothes, my socks and went to open the closet door. I was utterly flabbergasted, overwhelmed with emotion. My mother's satin-covered hanger, perched over the closet door, held a sweet green crepe dress, with a lovely sash. It was just my size, of course!! "Mommy, Mommy, what have you done? Did you cut apart your special dress? When did you make it? Why did you make it, Mommy?"

As she spooned my oatmeal into the bowl she twinkled and said, "You needed a special dress dear, so after you went to bed I got busy at the sewing machine. Do you really like it? Will you feel good wearing it?"

I think I was the most elegant little girl in the Spelling Bee competition in Columbus, Ohio. I had great fun, standing before the judges, spelling so very correctly, in my bright green dress! All were eliminated except one rather chubby boy (two years older than me) and me…I was so sure I was going to win. I was "too big for my britches" though, as Grandma used to say. The judge pronounced, "Flying. Flying." With a perky toss of my curls I said, "Flying…flying—f-l-i-n-g—flying". In that disastrous moment I came to my senses, realizing that I had not spelled the word correctly. How bold! How saucy! How disgustingly presumptuous! The *runner-up* diploma was a tainted honor. I don't remember the trip home. I don't remember anything Miss Martin said to me. I can only remember how sad I was that I would have to report my failure to Mom.

Mom hugged me and took me on her lap smiling when I reported the experience. She said, "I'm glad you looked so pretty today, Lois, and know what? We know you can spell. That is enough for me."

# 7 MY LYING TONGUE (1936)

I'm amused and sometimes bothered by some peoples' thinking that missionaries are cut from a different pattern, implying that we can't do or never did anything wrong! Believe me!—I've talked with doting women who have given me their impression that I must have been an exemplary, perfect child. Wouldn't it have sounded virtuous for me to declare that they were right. But it wouldn't have been the truth.

I was eight years old when Mom said, "Lois, take a dollar from my purse and go to the corner grocery store. Buy one loaf of white bread and a quart of milk."

Skipping along to the store I felt confident and grown-up, but on the way home my bouncy skipping changed to melancholic shuffling. I dropped the change from the purchases and the coins rolled into the grate in the sidewalk! I had no idea where they went.

I opened the kitchen door slowly, knowing that Mom would scold me. Even then my flair for dramatics declared itself as I set the groceries down with a heavy sigh. Mom turned to me. Taking advantage of her attention, I widened my eyes, threw my hands into the air and exclaimed, "Oh, Mommy, am I glad to be safe at home. A big, bad boy grabbed my arm when I left the store and forced my hand open, and Mommy, he took the change from the dollar. I've run all the way home."

Mom put her loving arms around me and hugged hard. Somehow that hug didn't give me much comfort!

# 8 JUNIOR WASN'T PERFECT (1938-1945)

When Bill was eleven years old he attended a children's summer camp. There he became aware that God was calling him to some kind of future service. He usually was very sensitive to the impressions of the Holy Spirit and his heart was open to the instructions from God's Word.

But there were moments when his stubbornness took over! Dad Miller liked his automobiles, even though they were always second-hand. He instructed his very interested son, "Don't you even think of trying to drive this car now. You're not old enough."

But Junior knew all about the shifting and the steering, the braking and the signaling. He was sure he could drive the car. He tried to get into the automobile, but every door was locked. Then he spied the baseball bat. The window on the driver's side was open just a wee crack at the top. Maybe he could wedge the small end of the bat into that opening and push the window down far enough to reach the door handle. Uumpph... uumpph the small end of the bat fit into the opening. So the boy pushed with all his might. The glass broke! Dad Miller came running. Junior ran, too. But he didn't get away from the punishment. Evidently it was an effective lesson. He never tried anything like THAT again!

Later another camp experience gave Junior the opportunity to hear from God. There he knew for certain that God called him to preach the Gospel full-time. Gone was the idea that he'd be a good medical doctor. Gone was the idea that he could make money and give some of it to God. Gone was the idea that he could choose his own way. He began to sing the song that was his parents' favorite: "God's Way is the Best Way." (Bill and I still like to sing it today.)

To be called "Junior" soon became inappropriate. Bill went away to Mt. Union College in Alliance, Ohio. He stayed at the Sigma Nu Fraternity House. All the resident boys were either going to be preachers or doctors, it seemed. They were moral and ethical in their relationships, but not all of them knew the Lord as personal Savior. The fellows didn't make fun of Bill, though, because of his testimony. He was always firm, but not in any way aggressive or judgmental. His friend, Tim, was not like Bill. Tim called attention to what he thought was his spiritual superiority, so the boys decided to teach him a lesson! I'm glad that Bill didn't participate in the set-up! (He was too busy working at odd jobs like mowing lawns in order to pay for his books.)

Under Tim's bed the fellows rigged up a little speaker connected to a microphone in the basement. They knew that Tim always had very lengthy devotions before going to bed. Just as he was getting under the covers a spooky-kind of male voice declared, "Tim, I need you. I need you, Tim." The fellow looked around, turned on the lamp, went to the window, listened at the hall door, saw nothing, and heard no one. He settled into bed and was startled by that same voice, "Tim, this is God. Answer me, son. I need you." Tim began to shake. He fell to his knees with a thud, crying out, "Oh, God, here I am, just like little Samuel, here I am, Lord." He started to cry. Then, in the quietness of the night he heart soft whisperings and controlled laughter. Then guffaws filled the room and the boys gave away their secret.

Partly because of such shenanigans Bill was impressed to take God and His commands very seriously. He knew God *"needed"* him (wanted him) in some pulpit somewhere. So he asked for opportunities to preach. He smiled with amusement when he told me the story of his very first sermon. He fluctuated between the Old and New Testaments for his text but finally decided what to preach. At last the sermon was done, written in longhand, ready for delivery. It seemed long enough. The next Sunday morning the congregation looked expectantly at the very young, pale-faced college boy. Bill slid his papers on the pulpit, cleared his throat, and sighed audibly. His voice sort of squeaked out the Scripture verses. With the Bible reading he gained confidence. He gave the whole sermon, feeling that he was in the right place. He closed in prayer and sat down. Then he looked at the clock. He had only preached six minutes! But it was a beginning.

# 9 FOR GOD SO LOVED LOIS (1938)

Don Seitman, home from Moody Bible Institute, knocked on our door. When my mother opened the door a smiling Don invited the children to attend a Sunday afternoon Bible Club. Mom answered firmly, "No, my daughters can't go." (She feared that Dad would be angry about that.)

Would you believe that Don returned six times more! Finally, because he invited us so insistently Mom agreed that he could come by for Charlotte and me to be taken to his parents' house the following Sunday. My sister and I had spasmodically attended Sunday School in a nearby church but were not aware of the need for a personal relationship with Jesus Christ, the Savior.

"Running over, running over…my cup is full and running over. Since the Lord saved me I'm as happy as can be; my cup is full and running over."

I sang the words to the chorus without knowing what "*saved*" meant. Pastor Nika gave the Bible lesson the third afternoon of the classes. He smiled down at me and asked, "What's your name, girlie?"

"Lois," I replied.

"Well, Lois I have a special message for you and all the boys and girls here. If you have your New Testament turn to the Gospel of John, the third chapter. I'll read the sixteenth verse like this: *'For God so loved Lois that He gave Lois His only begotten Son that if Lois believes in Him Lois will not perish, but have everlasting life.'* That means that Jesus gave His life for each of you today."

He went on to explain it so sweetly that my heart was thoroughly convinced that I needed to be saved. I felt too shy to raise my hand when Don gave an invitation. I was quiet on the drive to my home. Later, in our little bedroom, Charlotte and I were getting ready for bed. I could resist the tug on my heart no longer. I dropped to my knees beside our bed. Charlotte thought I was playing a new kind of drama-game. (I was often pretending new plots or acting out old fairy tales.) She laughed and started to tickle me. Nevertheless, I kept on talking to God silently and confessed my sin and accepted Jesus as my personal Savior. No special feeling flooded my soul. I sighed and crawled beneath the sheets.

But three or four nights later, under the bright stars and a gorgeous full moon, I carried the bag of trash out to the street. As I turned I looked up in the night and thought about the God who created all that beauty up there Who was now my personal God! I belonged to Him through Jesus, my Savior. I got excited. The Holy Spirit gave an effective, emotional witness to my soul.

# 10 MY FIRST VOCAL SOLO (1949)

"You, the one in the middle, please come over to the piano."

Johnny Hallet, pianist for the Children's Bible Hour, then said, "Sing something for me."

Trembling with nervousness I sang "What a Friend We Have In Jesus." What was I doing in the WHK radio studio in downtown Cleveland early on an October Saturday? I was twelve years old. I'd been a Christian a very short while.

This is how it happened. Rose and Vonnie, two of my Sunday School friends, invited me to form a trio with them. I sang the second soprano part. All our listeners always remarked about our harmonious blend. When we heard that Children's Bible Hour out of Grand Rapids, Michigan (still on the air today) was coming to our city to audition local youngsters for new talent, we gladly sent in our registration form. We arrived at the studio at 7:30 a.m.—the very first ones—flushed and giggly, but sure of our rendition of "On the Jericho Road." We sang well but were unhappy with the director's statement, "Sorry, girls, we already have a couple of trios."

Just then the pianist spoke up. After I sang a stanza of the hymn he startled me. "Here, look at this music. I'll play it for you."

I learned it right on the spot as he played, emphasizing the melody. We went over it twice.

I sang it at ten o'clock on nationwide radio—MY VERY FIRST VOCAL SOLO.

Since that song, *Jesus is Nearer and Dearer To Me*, I've kept on singing, singing, SINGING!

Rose Marie Weiss later married and went to the Philippines as a missionary with her husband. She died of cancer. Vonnie (Yvonne) Sanborn married Dr. Donald Waite and serves the Lord with him in New Jersey.

## 11 OCCASIONS FOR SINGING (1944)

I'll always remember Miss Gibson, the music teacher. She motivated me to sing well, with good *stage presence* and control. She encouraged me to participate in the High School Music Competitions. The very first oratorio solo I sang was on that high school stage, performing *O Rest in the Lord* from Mendelssohn's *Elijah*, for which I received a "Number One" rating. An indelible musical highlight was singing in the chorus comprised of students from different schools, presenting One World on the stage of the Cleveland Auditorium under the direction of Robert Shaw. Although a newcomer on the musical horizon he was already an acclaimed conductor. Wow!

Another experience that prepared me for learning to serve the Lord in music from the platform happened when Evangelist Torrey Johnson came to that same auditorium with Stratton Shufelt as his soloist. For some reason I was standing right in the front row, in the center, of the large volunteer choir. Strat Shufelt rehearsed us and then turned to me, and *scared the wits out of me* saying, "Please come here." He handed me a sheet of music, *Cleanse Me* and said, "I'll sing the melody. You do the obligato above me. Can you do that? I heard your voice and think you'll do a good job".

I didn't know whether to laugh or cry but there was no time for any excessive emotion. The curtain would open soon. We practiced the first line. He held up his hand and declared, "You'll do."

Every night, when the curtain opened, fifteen-year-old Lois Jean Pankuch went to the mic beside the celebrated Stratton Shufelt and sang her obligato part. (I had a battle with pride because of my response to that honor.)

## 12 I KNEW I'D NEVER MARRY (1947–1948)

Who was I to think that a good-looking, dedicated Christian gentleman like Bill Miller would look at me with smoldering eyes of love? I have never felt glamorous, not even pretty. In fact, as teenagers, when my sister Charlotte stood before the mirror we shared, she blurted out as she primped, "What a shame, Sis, all you have is brains!"

So, although I had three or four dates in high school, I wasn't convinced of any particular physical loveliness. But I don't remember worrying about my lack of outward beauty. Mom often said, "Pretty is as pretty does." As a Christian teenager my priority was learning to serve the Lord.

I went to Cleveland Bible College and had lots of men friends but no dates! I sang all the time—when I was invited for campaigns and revivals, when I represented the school on weekends, when I sang at Youth for Christ rallies, and when I performed my *domestic duties* on Saturday mornings in the college. One Saturday morning in early May of 1947 the administration building was empty. I was singing at the top of my voice while scrubbing the stairs. (I was referred to as *the girl with the built-in P.A. system*.) A courteous gentleman interrupted me, asking, "Could you please tell me where I can find Alice Ann Miller?"

After I gave him the directions to the piano practice room and told him my name, he said, "I'd be happy to have you come to my church in Orrville and sing in our services some Sunday soon. We'll have to arrange it."

I smiled and answered, "Let me know when I can do that."

"That will be good. By the way, I'm Alice Ann's father."

Alice Ann was my partner as we traveled in the college concert choir tour. Over and over again she described her wonderful older brother, emphasizing his desire for a wife "with musical gifts, long hair, a pretty smile and most of all, who loved and served God." So she cooperated well with Dad Miller in arranging a weekend for me to sing in Orrville. Then she said to her older brother, Bill, who was meeting her in Cleveland to go down together on the train to Orrville, "Please meet my friend at the rear of Taylor's Department Store. She has long brown hair, a nice smile, and she'll probably be wearing a blue suit or a black skirt and white blouse. She's going home with us."

I'll never forget what Bill wore that day—brown and white saddle shoes, blue trousers, a blue, yellow, and white plaid sport coat, a yellow tie and white shirt! His smile captivated my heart. He and I talked as though we were old friends and immediately found things in common: our love for the Lord, classical music (especially Bach, Handel, and Mozart), traditional hymns sung a cappella, libraries, and startling sunsets. God used that encounter with Bill and the circumstances of that weekend to change my philosophy. I had thought I would never marry. I was too independent! And I didn't feel I was attractive enough to please a man! When I returned to Cleveland that Sunday night I called Mom and surprised her with the words, "I met the man that if he had said, *Come away and marry me*. I think I would have done it. Mom, he's so wonderful!"

That Sunday morning in Orrville, Ohio I sang in the First Methodist Church where Dad Miller was pastor. Because the Millers had other guests the noon meal was quite festive. The whole time I was painfully aware of Bill's eyes upon me. I could hardly look into his expressive blue eyes without blushing.

After dinner Bill invited Alice Ann and me to accompany him to Mount Union College in Alliance (about forty minutes away) to pick up his belongings for the summer period at home. Alice Ann made sure I sat in the middle, between them. We sang in harmony the whole trip. Just as we pulled up to the first traffic light in town a chic, good-looking girl driving an open, white convertible in the next lane called out, "Hi, Bill, nice to see you in town. Do you have time to stop by the house for a Coke?"

Bill smiled, "Sure, Pat, why not?"

Alice Ann gave him a suspicious look. I reacted, too, but only on the inside, asking myself, "Who is this sophisticated girl? Is she his sweetheart?"

I felt ill-at-ease in her black, white, and chrome apartment. She *gushed* over Bill and served us Cokes and pretzels. Just as I raised my glass from the little silver tray I spilled my Coke on Pat's white shag carpet! She cleaned it without a fuss. And then offered to sing one of her recital songs for us. She sat at her white piano and sang adequately in a flute-like soprano.

Later that night Bill drove Alice Ann and me to the Bible College in Cleveland. I wondered, "Will he call me? Will I see him again? Did I imagine our instant attraction? Is Pat important to him?"

Later I learned that Pat was only the daughter of the doctor whose lawn Bill mowed each week. She was interested, but Bill was not!

The following Saturday I was scheduled to sing for a wedding. On Friday, Bill called me, "I want to come to Cleveland to see you tomorrow night."

And that is what happened for six consecutive weeks. Each time he came to Cleveland I was scheduled to sing for a wedding, a rather romantic atmosphere for developing our relationship. We chatted and got better acquainted as he drove me to my home. That sixth *date* is etched in my memory. On our way to the parking lot the summer downpour drenched our fancy clothes. In my parents' quiet living room Bill put his arms around me—our first kiss! But oh, I could hardly bear the odor of his wet wool Scottish tweed coat. It repelled me. The kiss was far from ideal! But it was a beginning. Two wedding songs and a concert date later I was convinced that God was going to put us together. Bill said nothing. His smoldering eyes spoke volumes.

He went to Pennsylvania to be best man for his college friend's wedding. I received a sweet letter. The closing sentence gave me goose bumps! "When I get back to Ohio I want to talk to you about some important things. All my love, Bill."

The following week I was rehearsing music at a friend's house. Mom phoned me there and sounded almost frantic, "Lois, Bill is down at the train station. He's between trains on his way back from Pennsylvania and he wants you to get down there right away."

I ran to the bus stop. When the bus arrived at the downtown square I bolted straight into Bill's arms. We sat at the drug store, talking about many things, holding hands and looking deeply into each other's eyes, but not declaring our love in so many words. We were so engrossed that he missed his train! So we waited for the next one. And talked and talked and talked. And he missed that one! The last one! The only thing then, was for Bill to come out to my house and spend the night on the sofa!

We sat on the porch swing for a while. Barbie, my four-year-old sister, climbed up on Bill's lap, stroked his chin affectionately and said, " Bill, when ya goin' ta marry Lois?" He quietly replied, "I'm really thinking about it, honey."

A few minutes later Bill excused himself and went to look for Dad. When he returned Barbie had gone to bed and we two were alone. On that memorable night Bill gave me his Sigma Nu fraternity pin. I was *pinned*. Engaged to be engaged!

We wrote to each other every day and on some Sundays Bill wrote two letters! We were really getting better acquainted. Thanksgiving was a very special day for us. Ruth, Bill's older married sister, lived with her pastor-husband in a large parsonage not very far from Cleveland. The whole Miller family gathered at their house that year. I joined them, feeling nervous about meeting everyone. But I loved them all, especially Grandma Youngberg, whose laughter was entertainingly infectious.

We continued writing our daily letters. On Christmas Eve, Bill arrived at our house. His smile, his hug, his kiss, all made me feel so cherished! (And beautiful!) After dinner the children danced up to bed. Dad was trying to assemble a tricycle, sighing audibly the whole hour. Mom was trying to quiet colicky Johnny, my baby brother. His fussy whimpering almost ruined the romantic setting Bill was creating. But not quite! A small diamond ring with little baguettes thrilled my heart. I asked, "How did you ever buy this?" (Later I learned that he had scrubbed floors at midnight in a restaurant near the college.)

After Christmas, Bill came to Cleveland twice. The daily letters continued. Then on Easter Sunday he received a student-pastorate appointment to a country church about forty miles south of Cleveland. Every Sunday morning very early, Bill drove about sixty miles to my home together we drove the forty miles to Pittsfield in time for the Sunday School hour at ten o'clock. After the morning worship, dinner with one of the members, and an afternoon of pastoral visitation together, we drove back to Cleveland. He usually left my home near midnight!

Those weekends of April, May, and June were our real bonding experiences. We had a favorite spot on the edge of Cleveland under some old oak trees where we parked and talked about our future, our dedication to God's service, our likes and dislikes, and expressed our good-bye for the week.

The wedding was set for July 2, 1948, a Friday afternoon. We were very young, very much in love, and very sure it was God's will for us to be together. I was no longer the independent girl who thought she'd never marry! But one of my friends, a pastor's wife, exhorted me with great concern, "Lois, Bill is a Methodist. There aren't very many Methodists who really preach the whole Gospel. Dear, I wonder if you are not in error? Get real serious about this step!"

The ceremony was to be simple and the reception following, very simple, too. Dad Pankuch didn't feel it was very necessary to spend much money on the bride. But a good marriage does not depend on an elegant wedding, a glamorous bride, or an expensive reception. Dad even stated in no uncertain terms, "Nobody's gonna get me into that church!"

But less than a week before the big day he softened and agreed to take me down the aisle. The wedding photograph reveals his fright, for he hadn't been in a church since he was fifteen years old!

My high school friend, Gigi, was my maid of honor; Alice Ann and my sister Charlotte were my bridesmaids; my little sisters, Nancy and Barbara, were the shy apprehensive flower girls. Gratian, the organist and Norene, the soloist, were sentimental pals from high school days. Bill's best man was his college buddy, and John Knox (sister Ruth's husband) and another college friend were the ushers. Dad Miller assisted the Reverend James Norton, my pastor, in the ceremony. Of course, my tears choked my voice when I said, "I do."

Sunday morning dawned bright and sunny. The bride and groom went to Bill's first resident pastorate, a two-church charge, Brighton-Rochester, near Wellington, Ohio. I wore the light blue linen suit that Aunt Bonita had lovingly sewn for me. When the lay leader introduced the new pastor and his bride I stood to my feet, but with difficulty. The men had painted the church and varnished the pews that past week in honor of the new bride. My nubby linen dress stuck to the varnish. What an introduction! Of course the fuzz could be sandpapered off the pew, but nothing could repair my new suit.

And that's the story of the bride who thought she'd never marry. I found a very good blessing in Bill Miller! He says that a wife doubles a man's pleasures and divides his cares.

## 13 OUR FIRST YEARS TOGETHER (1948-1953)

One weekend soon after our *inauguration* at the Brighton-Rochester charge, we nervously prepared for the district superintendent's visit. Saturday afternoon I dusted the house and then called upstairs to Bill, "I'm coming up now to clean your study, Honey."

It wouldn't take long. He only had three pieces of furniture: an old kitchen chair, a desk made of vegetable crates and an old door, and a small bookcase. Upon entering his room I let out a shout, "Uh-oh. What's the matter with you, Bill? How can you expect me to clean this room when you have a hundred books, opened and scattered all over, even on the floor?"

Bill replied in his calm, sometimes irritatingly quiet manner, "This is MY ROOM; I do what I need to do here and I need all these books open like this. I'm preparing my sermon, remember?"

"Well, then, prepare it in a dusty room!"

And I stomped down the stairs to our bedroom, I sat on the bed, sniffling into my dust rag! "How could he treat me this way? I've got to have the house clean for the D.S. What will I do? I married such a stubborn man."

I spouted out to God about my dilemma, but as I prayed He convicted me. I rose from my *martyr's seat* and started up the stairs toward my husband. Bill was coming down! We met about halfway, forgiving each other with hugs and kisses. In fact, we became so absorbed in loving each other that I never got up to dust the study! (The district superintendent wasn't at all interested in climbing the stairs the next day.)

We learned a strong lesson that day. We don't let anything *fester*. We endeavor to make things right soon after the incident. The wronged one doesn't have to wait for the offender to initiate the reconciliation. So therefore, we are able to maintain a loving attitude. Sometimes it takes longer than other times. I'm still emotional and Bill is still stubborn (sometimes—actually, very few times) but we don't want to allow things to mar the beauty of our relationship.

When I was still in my parents' home, my jobs were caring for the babies, scrubbing the upstairs bathroom, and going to the open market for vegetables and special sausages that could be obtained there. Mom very rarely wanted my help in the kitchen except to wash the pots and pans! So when Bill and I married Dad thought he was being funny when he told Bill, "Lois doesn't even know how to burn water!"

Cookbooks are marvelous possessions. I studied mine, anxious to please my new husband. Our budget was very, very, VERY limited. I used my ingenuity every day. I picked fresh, tender dandelion greens for our supper. When the budget was especially low I even used the young dandelion blossoms, dipped them in egg and flour and fried them—not too bad! I even sautéed cucumbers and radishes that the farmers brought us!

I aimed to make bread and thus save money, which would make my Bill happy, too. The recipe was easy to understand. I followed the directions. Soon the fragrance of baking rolls filled the whole house. I was excited! Bill sat down at the table, picked up the warm roll, smiled at me expectantly, and lifted the *bride's production* to his mouth. But his teeth could barely penetrate the hard roll. What had happened? I really don't know. I only know that after my first sensation of hurt feelings and then disappointment, I laughed along with Bill as he attempted to persuade Mergatroid, our little mongrel, to enjoy the warm roll. She refused, slinking under the table, ashamed for rejecting the offer. Bill chuckled, grabbed a few rolls, and went to the back door. A bull's eye decorated the garage door. He pitched one and then another, having fun with my baking!

The next batch of rolls were not only soft and fragrant—they were absolutely delicious. I'm not sure which lesson we learned from that episode. Probably just to polish our sense of humor.

Toward the beginning of autumn I began to think about a lullaby. I was pregnant. (Today's young people say, "WE are pregnant," but I was the one with morning sickness.) We prayed about the finances. Anxiety about the cost bothered my sleep; but Bill, the dreamer, and the faith prayer warrior was sure we'd pay for it all somehow. By the end of the third month I was no longer worried, just singing and expecting. I could hardly wait to wear a maternity smock. But harsh disappointment slapped us in the face! Bill rushed me to the hospital because of a spontaneous abortion (miscarriage) which the doctor explained, "Well, these things happen. Perhaps the baby would have been abnormal in some way. You'll have more opportunities." Somehow that didn't help my hurting heart.

During our first eleven years of marriage we learned much about patience and disappointment–six pregnancies were begun, but only resulted in one full term baby.

We lost one baby at Olivet Nazarene College in Illinois. Then, again, while we were back in Cleveland (now Malone College in Canton, Ohio) our anticipation almost unbearable. By remaining in bed most of the time I was able to avoid the miscarriage threat. I still had the list of those twelve children we had been expecting to raise as our family. Out of all the names we selected we used only one name. After my suffering frightening eclampsia, William George Miller III was delivered by Caesarean section. I cried to see my baby, but the nurse gently informed me, "He's very little and not too strong so the doctor has put him in the incubator. You'll see him tomorrow or the next day without a doubt."

Frankly, I was a bit taken aback by our baby's looks. He was so wrinkled. The nurse's aid whispered, "We call him the little monkey." Thankfully, he grew up to be a rather handsome guy!

## 14 NO MORE MIGRAINES (1948)

I had never seen a person suffer with migraine headaches before marrying Bill. As I stood before the bed seeing him cover his light sensitive eyes as he groaned with pain, my heart hurt for him. We were on the second floor of a cheap hotel in an unfamiliar town.

How did we get there? It was over twenty-five miles from our little parsonage.

We left our house about two o'clock that afternoon to make some pastoral visits in the country. About a mile from the house we were shocked to see an elderly man stooped almost to the pavement beside the road. Of course we had to stop. His heavy beard was full of little twigs and dead flies! His eyes were bloodshot: the hairs of his nose were clogged with dirt. Bill asked him, "Where are you going? What are you doing way out here?"

The man's quivering voice informed us that he was on his way to the County Rest Home. "There's no other place for me now," he said.

God changed our plans. With the man's sack behind us, we three crowded into the front seat of the car headed for Norwalk, the county seat. We talked to Gus about the Lord, about being prepared for eternity, and urged him to get right with God. He knew the Way, he said. Just then the car lurched, sputtered, gave a loud "clunk" and stopped. We put Gus under a tree beside the road and pushed the car onto the shoulder. I was ready to cry. Bill stood beside the highway, his hitchhiker's thumb high. Finally a state trooper came by. Seeing the old man beneath the tree, he stopped, and said, "You folks need help, right?"

We had waited quite a while beside the road. There was no bus to Brighton so the trooper took us to the hotel. He then delivered Gus to the County Rest Home.

Bill called our lay leader who assured us that he'd be there the very next morning. We lay down on the lumpy mattress. We had only two dollars which we didn't feel free to spend on food. The dim light bulb made me fell dismal. Bill said, "I've got to try to sleep. My head is aching terribly."

Soon the migraine attacked him mercilessly. I felt unable to help but I really wasn't helpless. I had the Lord. I knelt down beside the bed, took Bill's hand between my hands and prayed very simply, "Oh, Lord, You are Savior, Healer, Friend. Please touch Bill. Take away the pain. Heal him, please. Have mercy. In Jesus' name. Amen."

I stood by the window praying silently. About twenty minutes later Bill declared, "Honey, God has touched me. I'm O.K."

We thanked the Lord and celebrated with two big glasses of water. Praise the Lord!

Bill had suffered with migraine pain all during his young adult years. Since that incident in Norwalk he has had no migraine headaches. In fact, he very rarely has any headaches at all.

# 15 DISAPPOINTED (1949)

While Bill studied part-time at Ashland College and cared for the Brighton-Rochester charge, we were conscientious to be faithful in doctrine and love for our people. Over twenty young people came to know Christ as personal Savior during the first ten months we were there. God gave us the desire to bring the Wednesday evening prayer meeting back to life and to resurrect the Sunday evening service too. Then came the shock! Our lay leader, with an embarrassed stammer, announced that the District Superintendent would arrive the following Sunday evening for a "specially-called congregational assembly." My questioning glance at Bill received no response. He just said, "thank you" and dismissed himself to go upstairs to his little study. He had an inkling of what would happen.

Sunday night, all the older members of the congregation sat in their accustomed pews. Their offspring filled the back rows as usual. After some opening remarks, the superintendent turned to Bill and me, and I'm sorry to say, said in a condescending manner, "Pastor, the congregation and I have conferred. We want to say the following to you: Cancel the open testimony times in your services because they are embarrassing. We would prefer you transfer to Oberlin College for your studies now. It won't be necessary to continue the Wednesday evening meetings. At the coming Conference, you can transfer to the Kentucky conference where there are churches that would cooperate with your fanatical tendencies."

Bill had already investigated the studies at Oberlin College where the theology students were required to present a paper discounting the virgin birth. He would have no part of that. After an exchange of genteel but barbed phrases from several members, Bill was given an "ultimatum." For these reasons, he resigned from that pastorate.

We were perplexed and very disappointed. Why would we have to leave a ministry that had produced almost double growth in less than a year? The following Tuesday morning I was organizing the packing of our scant possessions. Our very dear friends, retired Nazarene China missionaries, Leon and Emma Osborne, knocked on our door. Bill and I had cried with the young people in their sorrow for our having to leave. I thought I had no tears left. However, Emma had to give me her handkerchief and pat my shoulder in Christian affection as we shared our disappointment with them. Because we had shared with them our dilemma they graciously felt they should help us.

Within one week's time we were installed in the empty upstairs apartment of the building where the Wellington Church of the Nazarene held services. Bill got a part-time job in a donut shop so we could eat. We both participated in the visitation program and the music ministry of the little church.

About three months later, while we were preparing for bed, there was an urgent pounding on the door. There stood Kent and Alice from Rochester, along with a crowd of the newly converted young people, overflowing with joy. They bounded into our empty living room and flopped to the floor.

"You'll never guess what happened tonight! We've got a student pastor from Oberlin, and he doesn't know beans about the Bible. We've been telling him about our saving faith in Jesus and tonight he said, 'I'd like to have that kind of experience,' so we led him to Christ just like you taught us."

During those lean months of transition I often cried. I asked questions too big for my brain. I wondered how my husband, so clearly called to the ministry, had to bear such ignominy and humiliation. I came to realize that I had lost the sense and sight to see God working in our circumstances. God is so big–and He WAS WITH US as well as the pastor that followed us into Kingdom purposes.

One day I opened our last can of food, nothing but plain corn. I heated it and served it to Bill who was preparing to go out with a classmate on a visitation program. Glen, his classmate, arrived just as we were praying at the lunch table. He observed the meager fare and joked, "Hey, God owns the cattle on a thousand hills. Why not ask Him for a side of beef? It sure would hit the spot!"

He was poor, too. Bill grinned and replied, "Well, Glen, I'll let you pray now and ask Him."

Glen did just that. The men left and I started to wash the forks and plates. The doorbell jolted me out of my daydreams of a succulent roast and baked potatoes. Adele, the farmer's wife from Brighton, stood in our hallway with a huge blood-stained newspaper-wrapped package. She smiled shyly and held it out for me to receive.

"Come in, come in. What is this?"

"Oh, I can't stay, Lois. My husband is waiting in the truck. We butchered early this morning and decided to bring you this piece. It should serve for four or five meals."

Tears filled my eyes. It didn't matter that the package stained my apron. I was dumbfounded.

"You and your husband were so faithful in your loving visits to me when I was in the mental hospital. This is one small way I can say thank you for your prayers and patience with me. Now that I'm well, I see God's hand in every happening in my life, thanks to you."

I could hardly wait for Bill and Glen to return. The next day we joined Glen and his wife for one of the most delicious meals of our lives—roast beef, baked potatoes, and sweet corn. Who needed anything more?

A few months later Bill and I tearfully left the small group of believers in the Wellington church. The Lord had given clear instructions to study at Olivet Nazarene College in Bourbonnais, Illinois near Kankakee, now Olivet Nazarene University.

When I think back on the experiences of those months, I remember our friend, Gordon Barnett. He stressed that when life gives us sour lemons, God makes sweet lemonade.

We lunched with Phyllis and her mother in Brunswick, Ohio in June, 2000 and she glowingly reported that the experience of the roast beef has stayed with her all these years as a lesson in God's provision. She repeated Philippians 4:19.

*But my God shall supply all your need
according to his riches in glory by Christ Jesus.*

## 16 LESSONS FROM "THORNS"
### (1952) Names of parishioners are changed

It is amusing, most often frustrating, how God purposely uses problem-making people to teach us lessons of compassion and patience.

Isabella was one of those persons in one of our first pastorates in a suburb of east Cleveland before going into the field. For many years she had been receiving counseling and medicine from a psychiatrist in the area. She loved coming to church. After the service, she endeavored to monopolize our attention. Bill and I took turns listening to her groans and complaints. Her body odor was nearly unbearable. When we talked, I would move back a bit to avoid the bad breath and the odor, but she would move forward pushing her face closer and closer. After everyone had left and Bill was locking the church doors, Isabella still talked on, moving to the outside sidewalk. Her coat hung crookedly on her round shoulders and her spotted felt hat, a little askew, gave her a rakish look. Did she understand our replies to her complaining comments? Was she sure of her salvation? She seemed to have no prick of conscience to lie so we were never sure if she really did read the Scripture passages we suggested. She was fearful to pray aloud, but she would repeat a simple prayer after us. Was she aware of our sacrifice to give her attention? Twelve months of Isabella resulted in our new awareness that Jesus was pleased with our giving His love to one of "the least." When she slipped into eternity we thanked God that Isabella had known the value of meeting with His people.

Another thorn God used to prepare us for future encounters was Celia, a young married woman who had been brought up in the church. For some reason unknown to us, she developed a strong jealousy toward me, the naïve wife of the pastor. One Sunday morning, I was bothered by some strange looks from the women and the pursed lips of a few men. That afternoon I visited one of the matriarchs of the congregation with whom I felt sweet confidence. She revealed the situation. Celia was spreading an evil rumor about me. She was saying, "The reason Lois stands at the door beside her husband and smilingly grasps the hands of the men of the congregation is because she's been sleeping around. You notice, don't you, that she holds the fellow' hands much longer than the women's hands. She's not as sanctified as she says!"

When I tearfully told Bill about the malicious story, he hugged me hard and said, "We won't worry, dear. God is our Defender. He'll take care of it." That didn't give me much comfort at the moment. I was relieved when God moved us on.

How encouraging and how interesting though, that during our first furlough from Ecuador, Celia approached me in a women's meeting and asked for my forgiveness.

While Bill was taking additional courses at Cleveland Bible College and serving as part-time pastor (before we went to the field), we agreed to live in an upstairs bedroom with kitchen privileges in the home of an elderly couple. The little Evangelical Friends Church was not prosperous enough to provide an apartment for the pastor. The arrangement called for flexibility and adaptability. Our landlord had only two loyalties: their church and their son and his family. Through their son, who was music chairman in the church, I learned a new sense of surrender. Even though I was soloist for large rallies and conferences in downtown Cleveland at the time, I was not asked to sing solos in our church (except when Bill included that as part of his message or closing invitation).

One late afternoon in March, old Oscar (the landlord) and I were alone in the house. His wife was shopping and Bill was making home visits. I was in the kitchen to prepare our light supper. As I opened a drawer to get a paring knife Oscar sidled up beside me, grabbed the butcher knife and smiled strangely. I tried to make conversation but he stood woodenly beside the stove, his face puckered and jowly.

Just as I turned to put water on the vegetables he blurted out, "Don't do that. Stand over here. I need to kill you."

Had I heard correctly? He took one step toward me, lifting the knife into the air. I needed a quick injection of adaptability! I answered him softly, "Brother Oscar, I want to give you a special gift. Come sit by the piano."

I took firm, but slow steps into the dining room where his rocker filled the corner. The piano was on the opposite side of the room. A large oak table was between us.

God manipulated the scene. I played the piano very inadequately but managed to play and sing "Silent Night, Holy Night" as Oscar rocked rhythmically. My fingers trembled. Oscar stood, the knife held firmly in his right hand. I didn't hesitate. With sweaty hands and quaking voice I sang *"Oh, Come All Ye Faithful"*. Oscar's creaking rocking chair kept me aware that I needed help.

When I finished the carol and Oscar repeated the statement about killing me, I thought, oh Lord, where are you?

Oscar started toward me, mumbling the threat to use that knife. I sang, only able to repeat *"Silent Night, Holy Night."* During the last phrase, Oscar's wife opened the door, perceived the tension, dropped her packages, and rushed to Oscar's side. I kept singing. With her left arm around Oscar. she headed for the telephone. At that precise moment, Bill slipped in the back door, ascertained what was going on and called the police. I couldn't hear what he said on the phone in the kitchen because I was busy repeating *"Christ, the Savior is born,"* each time more weakly.

The police officers entered with two medical men. Oscar didn't want to give up the knife. I sang on—softly. The men wrapped Oscar in a straitjacket and carried him away, his wife by his side.

I collapsed into Bill's arms. We had no appetite that night for a light supper. Only a strong desire to thank God for divine care during that frightening hour!

## 17 GOD CARES FOR JALOPIES (1954)

Let me convince you that God's hand of care is extended towards even the small things. In 1954, Bill and I purchased a partially rusted 1941 Dodge. The little car had been driven almost 100,000 miles and the price was all we could afford—$80.00. Winona Lake Summer School of Theology was our destination and "Jalopy" purred her way to Indiana without a mishap.

As you know, dear reader, we had submitted an application to OMS for service in South America while we were in Indiana.

"Jalopy" returned us to Cleveland as we anxiously waited for the letter from mission headquarters in Los Angeles, hopefully containing the almost unbelievable news of our acceptance. It came two months and a few days after the application was submitted. Amazing! The persistent motor of our Dodge chugged its way to the Labor Day weekend camp where we were saturated with the need of the Latin Americans by Bill Gillam's stirring messages. Then, we launched out in deputation ministry on faith.

We were apparently calm on the outside. I was accustomed to singing both in the big rallies of Youth for Christ and in the Crusades and Bill had been preaching since he was 18 years old. In actuality, our knees were shaking, our hearts were pounding furiously, and our lips needed much moistening as we presented our first missionary service. The same was true of our second and our third! After each service we leaned back in "Jalopy" (that really was its name!), giving thanksgiving to the Lord.

As it carried us to our services, "Jalopy" heard prayers of consecration, exclamations of praise, and sighs of amazement at God's blessing.

One night the much-used car had to travel over a dusty, bumpy, deeply rutted detour. It chugged and clattered, sputtered and choked. We said to each other, "Well, that sounds like the end of 'Jalopy', doesn't it?"

But God surprised us! We traveled 13,000 miles more. It was as if the car cooperated, sensing something of our perseverance and determination! Or perhaps it was like the sandals in the desert that never wore out in the Old Testament story of the Jews travels in the wilderness. God's provision for them then and for us centuries later.

Seven months after our first deputation service, "Jalopy" carried us 170 miles to our last missionary meeting. We prayed at every indication of its balkiness. Thankfully we made it!

All our financial need was finally supplied. While returning home that evening to relate to Mother and Dad Miller our gratitude to the Lord, we were rudely interrupted by the Dodge's coughing and sputtering. We literally jolted our way home to Cleveland, praying that the car's wheezing motor would take us just five more miles, just four more miles, three more…on to West 98th Street, Cleveland. We gratefully parked our well-worn friend, "Jalopy", in front of the house. It really was finished this time. It sat there until it was towed away. We couldn't get even a sigh from the car that had carried us through Indiana, Kentucky, Ohio, and Pennsylvania, as we presented our need to get to South America.

That is why we say that God cares even for worn-out, rusty Dodges, especially when they belong to poor missionary candidates.

# 18 WHY DOESN'T HE ANSWER THE DOOR? (1955)

While Bill and I were in San Jose, Costa Rica, I was invited to sing in special church services or for functions at the Christian radio station. Bill would remain at home with baby Billy while I took the bus to my appointments. This often meant getting home when some streets were shrouded in darkness and the dim street lights barely penetrated the eerie shadows.

One night in autumn, I was returning from a meeting in the downtown church. It had been raining intermittently so I carried the black family umbrella. As I stepped down from the bus at our street corner, I noticed a man in the shadows across the street. I heard footsteps behind me. I looked around. There was that man! I wondered about that. Then he came so close I could hear his mumbling. I crossed to the other side of the street, avoiding the puddles, hoping the streetlight would shed some beams of security for me. He crossed the street, too. I quickened my pace. His steps grew more rapid. I ran into our yard and fell against the door, pounding hard on it. The man stood just about four yards from me, beside the gardenia bush. I knocked again and shouted. No answer! I looked up to see that the upstairs light was on and the shade was not pulled down. Bill HAD to be there.

"Bill is probably just absorbed in his Spanish lesson," I reasoned to myself and knocked harder and longer. Still no answer! "Oh, dear Lord, help me."

Then the man began speaking out obscenities that made my heart race. My mouth got drier and drier. I was so frightened! He threatened something very horrible, but he didn't approach me. I called out to Bill again. The man chortled. No answer from my husband.

"He must have gone to sleep. I'll go around to the kitchen door," I said to myself.

The back door was locked too. I rushed to the front door where the light beamed into the wet darkness of the scary night. I hollered and hollered again. It was beginning to sound more like a scream. Then I knew I had to do something drastic! I threw the umbrella up to the window where I thought Bill was sleeping, hoping I'd break the windowglass. That would startle my snoring husband! But no, the pointed end of the umbrella lodged in the soft wood of the clapboard next to the window frame and hung there, "zinging" up and down ridiculously as though to taunt me! The umbrella was stuck! I had no weapon then.

The man came close enough to touch me. He spoke in a low, threatening tone.

"Oh Lord, help me. Have mercy." I cried aloud.

At last, the front door opened slowly and my groggy husband said, "Honey, I'm sorry; I fell asleep."

I rushed at him, pounding on his chest, "Don't you know that wicked man almost raped me? Why did you lock the door? Why did you go to sleep? Why didn't you hear me yelling?" I kept on pounding! "Why didn't you come? Why?…why?…why?"

I railed until I was spent and Bill soothed me until I was finally able to sink down in the sweetness of relaxed sleep.

Two weeks later a "peeping tom" was arrested for alarming the women who lived in our neighborhood. The police were looking for him because of his history of sexual assaults.

Such episodes have to teach us some lessons I'm sure. "So what did you learn?" you ask?

First of all, each one ALWAYS carries the house keys.

Secondly, we don't fool around trying to find ways to get out of trouble. We call out to God IMMEDIATELY!

And thirdly, I have to improve my aim!

We were impressed that God had effectually protected me. At the time the man was arrested we received a letter from a prayer partner in Pennsylvania who had been praying for ME and for my PROTECTION during that month. I was thankful for the insight from the Holy Spirit and her obedience to cover me in prayer.

# ECUADOR

A fascinating country of contrasts and challenges...

# 19 LANGUAGE HURDLES (1955)

Missionaries have to communicate. Through acts of kindness and love, through living examples of courtesy and attention, but most of all, through what they SAY, in conversation, preaching, teaching, etc., in the language of their people. Without the language, the missionary is terribly hampered. I would go so far as to say that without using the people's language we could not have remained in the field. I'm not sure at this writing how many languages there are in the world. There are at least 1500 different cultures and thousands of languages and dialects. Bill and I could not be exempt from learning the language of "our people."

When we arrived in San Jose, Costa Rica to be enrolled in the Language School for Spanish, we were required to take language-aptitude tests. I was born with a quick ear for tones and sounds so the phonetics were quite easy for me. That is, until after I realized that the "rr" of Spanish is not produced by the muscles of the throat, but rather by the loose tongue tipping the palate in front of the mouth. When the vowels are pronounced correctly, the "rr" just comes out "automatically". I cried about it every day until I finally caught on. The Spanish grammar and vocabulary were no jolting problem because I had five years of Latin as an honor student for the supposedly "dead" language which is the foundation of all the romance languages.

But Bill, having studied the guttural German, always battled with the "rr" of the romance language. He was further troubled because his ear couldn't pick up the phonetic sounds. That surprised both of us because his fine sense of tone for the violin is nearly perfect.

The director of the school called us into his office when the results of the language aptitude test were disclosed. Bill's grade was not promising. In fact, Dr. La Porte rather ungraciously stated, "I'd suggest you make plans to find missionary service in English. You'll never learn Spanish, Mr. Miller."

My beloved is an obedient servant of the Lord. God had called us for foreign service. Who were we to doubt God? So Bill answered the director very courteously, "We'll stay. God is faithful who has called us. I'll work diligently and God will help me in this matter." Dr. La Porte shrugged his shoulders and dismissed us.

It is wonderful, wonderful, WONDERFUL that when God calls us, He equips us. In the varied facets of missionary service He does the preparing of His stewards. At the heart of our faith is the truth that God is sovereign. This means that God can choose however, whenever, and whomever He wants! He is not bound by what people might think is best.

God is not required to abide by conventional tests and evaluations. He can even make choices that some people may think are preposterous. We can trust God's leadership. He called us. He would take us through language school and equip us. We reminded each other of the verse that we had read, *"Whatsoever thy hand findeth to do, do it with thy MIGHT."* (Ecclesiastes 9:10) Our hands held the language books confidently!

By the time OMS asked us to leave Language School and take up responsibilities in Ecuador, after almost eight months of study, Bill's vocabulary was much larger than mine. He was able to read the Bible aloud more than adequately and was well on his way to conversing intelligently and preaching clearly in Spanish.

I made some unforgettable bloopers while we were studying. I qualified for the advanced level class because of the Latin I had studied. I was the only beginner woman student with nine missionary men who had all spent a term on the field and were "refreshing their memories." When it was my turn to give a little speech, the first one of the semester, I was excited as I stood before my classmates. My face was flushed with anticipation. I spoke out clearly, declaring, "Me pongo delante de ustedes muy embarazada." I thought I was saying, "I stand before you, feeling embarrassed." What I really said was, "I stand before you very pregnant." The fellows guffawed and the class was disrupted by this overly confident gal.

We arrived in Guayaquil on my birthday, December 27th, not ready to give any orations in Spanish, but not feeling intimidated. Our self-confidence was sorely pricked when John Palmer, our senior missionary, minutes before our first church service in Guayaquil, advised Bill he was to preside at the meeting. Bill went to the platform, smiled, and announced the hymn, saying, "Por favor, pies arriba." He thought he was saying, "Please stand to your feet." What he said was, "Please put your feet up." It didn't disconcert the people at all. They chuckled and stood. My reaction was, "Oh dear, the people are going to think we're stupid. We'll not have their respect. They'll not accept us."

God takes incidents like that and uses them in beautiful ways. The believers felt very kind and sweet toward Bill. His mistake and his humility over it endeared him to them. We had no problem. They accepted us. We were able to jump over the language hurdle.

# 20 THE AUCA INCIDENT (1956)

Only a very few of the Ecuador missionary personnel were aware of a strategy to go into the jungle of the Aucas. Bill and I, along with our OMS colleagues, didn't know about the five brave missionary men who joined forces to fly into Auca territory, landing on a beach of the Curaray River, until Bill and John Palmer heard the news on the ham radio. The missionary men knew that they had a very, very difficult task in trying to bridge between twentieth century and the stone age. The five men, Jim Elliot, Roger Youderian, Pete Fleming, Ed McCully, and Nate Saint (the pilot), dropped their photos to the Aucas to familiarize them with their faces. They established their base and made radio contact as scheduled with their wives. They reported the visit of Aucas but then no word came through on Sunday afternoon, January 8th. Marj Saint was in Shell Mera, responsible to pass word along to the other wives. Just after sundown on that Sunday, one of the medical doctors with the mission hospital came into the radio room and saw Marj slumped down on the desk. Elisabeth Elliot wrote:

> She told him the situation briefly, but asked that he not divulge it yet. If nothing serious had actually happened, it would be disastrous to publicize what was taking place… By seven o'clock on the morning of Monday, January 9, 1956, Johnny Keenan, Nate's colleague in the Missionary Aviation Fellowship, was in the air flying toward the sand strip which Nate had earlier pointed out to him.[1]

As he flew, Marj called Elisabeth in Shandia, saying, "We haven't heard from the fellows since yesterday noon. Would you stand by at ten o'clock for Johnny's report?"

The report came from Johnny, saying that he found the plane on the beach and that all the fabric was stripped off. There was no sign of the missionary men.

Bill and John received the radio message. News flashed around the world: "FIVE MEN MISSING IN AUCA TERRITORY." Bill helped relay the news to other ham operators. Those hours were tense for all of us. We were so far removed from the action. We didn't know personally any of the people involved, but when the news of their martyrdom was confirmed our hearts, hurt for the widows and their children. I remember looking at Geneva DeYoung with an enigmatic question in my eyes.

One week after the martyrdom of the missionaries we received the radio message that a memorial service was being held at the Bible Institute of Shell Mera.

Later, when I saw a couple of the widows, I was tongue-tied. I didn't know what to say and sat there in a cold sweat. Who was I to say anything adequate? Those precious women demonstrated the control of the Holy Spirit in their lives very forcefully. Barbara Youderian wrote in her diary:

> God gave me this verse two days ago, Psalm 48:14, *'For this God is our God forever and ever: He will be our guide even unto death.'* As I came face to face with the news of Roj's death, my heart was filled with praise. He was worthy of his home-going...I wrote a letter to the mission family, Trying to explain the peace I have...Roj came to do the will of Him that sent him...The Lord has closed our hearts to grief and hysteria, and filled it with His perfect peace.

Bill and I were new missionaries on the field and could not help but wonder if we could ever be so brave in the face of such tragedy. I was moved to pray for those five noble missionary women over and over again. One of the officials of the Rescue Service took the widows to fly over Palm Beach to see their husbands' graves. Elisabeth Elliot wrote about that experience:

The Navy R-4D took us out over the jungle, where the Curaray lay like a brown snake in the undulating green. Pressing our faces close to the windows as we knelt on the floor of the plane, we could see the slice of white sand where the Piper stood. Olive Fleming recalled the verses that God had impressed on her mind that morning: 'For we know that if our earthly house of this tabernacle were dissolved, we have a building of God, an house not made with hands, eternal in the heavens.' (He who has prepared us for this very thing is God.)...'Therefore we are always confident, knowing that, whilst we are at home in the body, we are absent from the Lord.'

As the plane veered away, Marj Saint said, "That is the most beautiful little cemetery in the whole world."

One of the Quichua Indians prayed that God would give the Aucas, instead of fierce hearts, soft hearts. "Stick their hearts, Lord, as with a lance. They stuck our friends, but You can stick them with Your Word, so they will listen, and believe."[2]

---

[1]. Quotations are from *Through Gates of Splendor* which is the full account of "Operation Auca", written by Elisabeth Elliott, published by Harper & Brothers, New York, 1976.

[2]. The Christian world rejoices today that now a sizeable number of the Wuarani are believers worshipping the Lord in the western edge of the Ecuadorian Amazonian jungle. Wuarani is the correct name of the tribe, the culture and language, as the word 'auca' is a quechua term employed by outsiders previous to 1987. 'Auca' actually means "savage" which makes it a derogatory term.

## 21 SIX PAILS AND TEN DISHPANS LATER (1956)

"Hurry, hurry," Ellen Sparrow yelled. "There's water all over the living room floor."

And sure enough, the heavy rains pelting against the balcony had come into the house. Edna Sparrow grabbed the mop, Geneva DeYoung hastened to the kitchen for the sponge. Tommy Sparrow and my husband got the dustpans and began scooping up the water. What fun! With shoes off and lots of chuckling, we all got to work. Stewart Sparrow looked so cute in his raincoat, trousers rolled up, no shoes, no socks, climbing out to unstop the balcony drain. Six pails and ten dishpans later the floor was almost dry. We flopped into the chairs and giggled.

Stewart and Edna Sparrow with their daughter Sharon, Ellen and Tommy, Geneva DeYoung, Audrey Kerr, and Bill and I with our toddler all lived in a huge apartment together in downtown Guayaquil, thus saving money so we could help reduce the field budget. During those months, we women shared kitchen supervision and we all learned more about interpersonal relationships to the glory of God. As I look back, I think that mopping up project was probably the peak of our sharing.

## 22 I GOT RID OF THE GARBAGE (1956)

In the autumn of 1956, Bill and I sat before the fireplace in a Quito guest house. Billy was tucked in for the night. Other guests were already in their rooms. We started to chat about Bill's responsibilities in ministry. He had been working so hard that he welcomed this short vacation in the mountains. I sputtered out to him, "Well, you can easily talk about being tired because of all your work, but I only play the piano in Philadelphia Church and help Geneva with the children's clubs. I'd like a ministry of my own! I'm really sad that I don't have a special responsibility that matters."

By this time, my eyes were filled with tears of frustration and disappointment, but most displeasing to the Lord were my tears of anger and self pity. Bill let me cry for a few minutes. Then he stroked my hand gently as he talked. "Listen to me, my love. Have you ever thought that maybe your resentment and bitterness concerning your Dad is an obstacle? Perhaps the Lord can't use you; maybe He doesn't trust a ministry in your hands because of those bad feelings. Those feelings are like festering sores. You've carried them around deep in your heart for so long. Why not face up to them once and for all?"

"What can you possibly mean?" I responded defensively. "Don't you remember how I told you I used to pray for Dad when I was at Bible College? I told you how my knees were calloused because of my kneeling on that rough old rug, praying for his salvation. I remember how I cried in prayer then, feeling sorry for Mom, and hating Dad's lack of interest in spiritual things. Hating how he spent money on horse races and football games, drunk almost every weekend, and other disgusting behavior."

"Mmmm, you've talked about that. But that is how many men without Christ live."

I didn't let Bill say anymore. I blurted out, "You know, don't you, how I feel around Dad? Most of the time I'm uncomfortable…so much so that I make little effort to say anything. I'd just rather leave him alone because I know I don't interest him. Nothing I've ever done has been important to him. I got Latin medals, received honors in school, sang in concerts. Oh, he should have been proud of me. Do you know that he never attended any function where I was recognized. He never even went to hear me sing? In fact, he never encouraged me to sing. I used to get so disturbed when Charlotte and I were doing the dishes, singing happily at the top of our voices, having fun and then Dad would holler out from the living room where he sat with his beer and pipe, 'Hey, cut out that noise and get to work!' It wasn't noise! Our voices sounded nice. That bothered me every time it happened. So many times. I fely awkward around him. Why do I have to go to him and say 'hello' for he never speaks first, and then why do I have to be the one to go to him to say 'goodbye?' That shows I'm not important to him! You remember how he didn't even want to attend our wedding! Mom had to beg him and he waited until the last few days to give us any assurance that he'd be there. He didn't show any interest in our call and preparation for the mission field, either. Remember that time when we went to the house and he immediately walked out the back door? He wanted to avoid us. My feelings are justified, if you ask me!"

"Mmmm, you've said that before, Lois."

I sat there, going over the memories and tasting the hurt all over again. It seemed that I didn't want to let go of the resentment because that would mean I would need to forgive Dad completely! I thought about that. Bill was quiet beside me.

I thought about those days when I prayed so fervently for Dad's conversion. I faced up to my unbelief. During those times my voice was pleading, "Lord, save Dad," but my heart kept up a stream of negative thoughts. "Dad will never yield to the Lord. He's too proud," I said to myself. That was so foolish! I thought of what the Bible says, "God's hand is not shortened that it cannot save."

Bill still had my hand in his. He patted it and sighed. An urge to pray overwhelmed me. I dropped to my knees then with my husband at my side. I started with the first memory of Mom's tears, confessed my bitter feelings about that and went on, praying and crying, remembering episode after episode, hating the horrible LACK OF FORGIVENESS I HAD HARBORED IN MY HEART! I became sorrowful for my sin...the lack of pardon. I had not ever pardoned him for anything. I kept remembering, remembering Mom's sacrifices and Dad's self-indulgence. Memory after memory. I let them go, telling God that I was sorry and asking His forgiveness. It was like taking the lid off a foul-smelling garbage can in the alley.

In my praying and sobbing I thought about that couplet we used to chant as children:

> "Sticks and stones may break my bones, but words can never hurt me." and sighed, saying, "That's not true. Dad's words (or sometimes lack of them) hurt me. It made me feel worthless, rejected, unloved."

Bitterness engenders more bitterness so there was much garbage to deal with. I tearfully prayed for a long time. Finally, after declaring my freedom in Christ and my victory over resentment and bitterness, I stood to my feet, wobbly and weak. That act of garbage disposal was debilitating, but I was no longer a victim, but a victor!

Free! Free! FREE!

I felt like dancing and leaping, shouting and singing.

Throughout the succeeding months the enemy of my soul tempted me, bringing up old memories. Even though much of the forgetting was impossible, the forgiveness had been declared. The devil had no accusation against me. It is difficult to forgive when one thinks she has suffered an injustice at the hands of another. I don't think it is possible to entirely forget even though one has forgiven. Letting go of the past and the hurts and anger is a matter of the will, but our brains remember! I realize that forgiveness does not imply that what others have done does not matter. Forgiveness really means the opposite. It doesn't minimize the seriousness. Forgiveness meant that I had to let go of the hurt.

It meant that I looked to God for healing that night.

The Lord has reminded me again and again that I am responsible for my attitude. That negligence to admit my unforgiving spirit rumbled around in the bottom of my heart for many years. Even when the joy of deputation ministry, language learning, and transition to the field was uppermost in my mind and feelings, underneath was that always present vexatious problem. Now I was free, gloriously and joyfully free. THERE IS REALLY NO JOY WITHOUT FORGIVENESS. I could genuinely praise the Lord, pleasing Him, because I had pardoned Dad and begun to love.

I communicated through a long letter my release from the bondage of unforgiveness and my act of love toward Dad. I thanked him for caring for my needs of food, clothing, and textbooks. In His time God answered my prayer regarding responsibility for ministry. Later Mom wrote that Dad began to read the Bible (surreptitiously). He listened to a radio program, "The Lutheran Hour" on which the Reverend Walter Maier clearly presented God's grace. Even later, the emergency treatment in the hospital for his asthma grabbed Dad's attention to his soul's need. He had also been listening to the Christian and Missionary Alliance radio program of south Cleveland. Soon he walked down the aisle to the altar in the church that sponsored that program and gave his heart to Christ in repentance. The Holy Spirit had done His work! It seemed that my obedience in releasing Dad from my UNFORGIVENESS contributed to opening the channel for God's message to get through to him. I had no "unfinished business" with Dad or with the Lord! There was no more garbage in my heart.

When I was going through letters and notes that Mom had kept for me, in case I would write a book, I found a letter that Dad had written to Mom from Madrid, Spain, where he visited with an M.F.M. witness team. I was profoundly moved by his words about ME! He wrote, "You would be very glad, honey, to know how much the people here love our Lois. She and Bill know how to reach out to people. That made me proud." How about that?

# 23 DON'T CRY, LET'S PRAY (1957)

Elenita's make-up was streaked because of her tears. As I listened to the heart-broken Ecuadorian woman's distress my heart responded with deep sympathy. Her husband's mistress had taunted Elenita in a downtown restaurant. When Elenita complained to her husband he laughed and replied, "Live with it, woman."

Her long list of hurts and disappointments tore at my emotions. We read some Bible verses and I prayed. Elenita had not yet come to saving faith in the Lord. She walked out so forlorn…so sad…so piteously depressed.

I sat in the living room, wiping away the tears for Elenita. Oh, I felt so sorry for her.

Billy was playing in the bedroom and heard my sighs and sobs. His three-year-old heart was touched and he ran over to me, climbed onto my lap, stroked my cheek and asked, "Why are you crying, Mommy?"

"Because my friend isn't happy in her home."

"Well, Mommy, don't cry. Let's pray."

Why did a toddler have to call my attention to the most wonderful activity for the saddened heart? We prayed. All day long I kept lifting Elenita to the Lord. It was a long time of affliction for her before her problem was solved, but she learned, too, that praying and trusting in the Lord is much better than holding on to sorrow and tears.

# 24 I LEARNED FROM GENEVA (1957)

The house was sitting upon long poles that looked like spindly legs, reaching down into the mud when the tide was in. I accompanied Geneva DeYoung to the children's classes in several areas of Guayaquil, but the most fascinating one was a class held out on the edge of the city. About fifty black-eyed boys and girls crowded into the split-bamboo house. I helped to teach them choruses and repeat Bible verses. I was excited when Geneva informed me, "Lois, you can prepare the Bible lesson for the children; here is the material."

Oh, how I practiced. I'm sure Bill was weary of Naaman and his many dips in the Jordan River! One memorable afternoon I went to the neighborhood on stilts with two Ecuadorians. The rain had made the wooden walkways very slippery. My tennis shoes made walking there worse. The Ecuadorians slipped on ahead and I was devastated. I began to slide. I held on to my portfolio and screamed as I went down, just a few inches from the slimiest mud you can imagine. God sent two helpful men from the Sanitary Department who were out spraying against malaria. One walked in front of me, holding one hand and the other walked behind me, supporting my elbow.

The next week they weren't there. I fell right down into the odiferous mess! Only the dogs, a parrot, a pig, and a braying donkey noticed me. Several months later a young mother from that area was converted in the OMS Berea Church. Her home became the center of evangelism for the neighborhood and later was called "Noah's Ark Church."

On Sunday afternoons, Geneva loaded up the teaching paraphernalia in the car and went to the Bible classes. As I observed her meticulous concern for the children and her faithful attention to them and their mothers, I learned more about servanthood.

# 25 BATTLE-SCARRED (1957)

In February, I wrote to my mother about a new experience, describing all the gory details.

I was battle-scarred! One Saturday night the closing program of the Daily Vacation Bible School in the Berea Church demanded all my attention. I played the little military pump organ.

Down by my feet, where the bellows are, it was dark. The mosquitoes love the darkness (I'm sure because their deeds are evil as the Scripture says!) A whole swarm met me when I sat down to play. The program was so arranged that there was a chorus or some kind of special song between each spoken part. I couldn't get away from the organ one minute. There were times while I was playing, that I actually shuddered from their biting and stinging. Not even thoughtful Geneva DeYoung had brought any spray. So I suffered, even though I had put on insect repellent before leaving the house. You can't imagine the torture!

The mosquitoes had a great banquet. After the program one child looked down at my bare legs and screeched, "Look at her bloody legs!" There were little blood drops on the floor in front of my chair. I hadn't leaned down to scratch, fearing that once I started scratching I'd not stop. Apparently they bit so much and so furiously that my skin didn't close up. I carried those battle itching battlescars around with me for some time.

## 26 THE FACTORY OF GOSPEL CHORUSES

Memories of dear Alfredo Colom Maldonado keep washing over my mind in unexpected wavelets. He authored thousands of gospel songs because of his deep devotion to the Lord whom he loved so vibrantly.

Alfredo, born in Guatamala, worked with OMS in Colombia first and then came to Ecuador. He was responsible for the radio program that we participated in. He took over the fledgling Berea Church, the second OMS church in Guayaquil, where we served as "apprentices" our first couple of years.

Alfredo would come to our house, grinning from ear to ear. Invariably, he had a new song to share or a new experience to relate. Bill and I learned a valuable lesson from him. We noticed that in all the evangelistic meetings and special services he held, he gave personal attention to those who came forward for prayer. And always—without fail—he sent a personal letter of encouragement with spiritual exhortation to each one. That kind of communication has been important for us too, as we've followed his example.

Alfredo's well-prepared messages were interrupted occasionally by a very mild, short seizure of epilepsy called petit mal in which he lost consciousness. Listeners would patiently wait those few seconds. Then Alfredo would resume his preaching.

His resonant voice and talent on the accordion were dimmed in his latter years by illness, including deafness, but his love and faith in Jesus never wavered. He was a wonderful, wonderful example for us.

He loved to write poetry for special occasions. When we left for a furlough one time, he wrote a poem dedicated to Guillermo y Loida Miller,

Siervos de Dios (William and Lois Miller, servants of God) containing fifteen verses! Is it any wonder that I hold him in my memory? I am blessed to sing one of his songs, now translated to English: (Cuan Felices Fuimos):

### HEAVENLY JOY IS RINGING

Heavenly joy is ringing and our hearts are singing,

For His blood hath bought us—when condemned, He sought us.

Men of every nation sing the great salvation

Of our blessed Jesus, who in mercy freed us.

Hail, Thou blessed Savior! We through Thee find favor;

Thou for us art pleading, ever interceding.

## 27 "STREAMS" TOUCHED DRY LIVES (1957)

The radio program, "Manantiales" (Streams) with Alfredo Colom in Guayaquil in 1957, blessed our hearts as God taught us some good lessons of perseverance in that evangelism endeavor. One day, just as my fingers danced down a keyboard, a fat rat bounded over to the piano and stopped for a second. Then, with singular grace, he walked across my feet on the pedals! Bill says I didn't miss a note. I don't know. I wondered how I ever remained calm.

That particular week of broadcasting, we were praying with great fervor that someone would come to Christ through the message and the music.

Later that month we received a long letter from a listener. Her story proved the answer to our prayers:

> My heart was darkened with resentment. My husband, drunk as usual, lay snoring in the loft overhead, while our nine children huddled on mats in the corner of our little house, taking their afternoon naps. I reasoned to myself that I was sick and tired of my fat, lazy, unfaithful, drunken man. My legs would just begin to heal from one beating and he'd grab a club again. I was tired of his mistresses and the evil women he strutted in front of me. Because the kids cowered every time he came home I thought we'd be better off without him.
>
> I took the butcher knife from the kitchen drawer and climbed the ladder. My husband snored louder and flopped over, flat on his back. I lifted the knife, but I

hesitated, 'Why can't I just plunge this thing into his chest? What's the matter with me?' I thought.

Again I tried to push the knife into his chest but I just couldn't do it. Just then the neighbor's radio penetrated my befuddled mind. The speaker said, 'Christ Jesus, Himself man, is between God and man, to bring them together by giving His life for all mankind.' I choked back a bitter sob and put the knife back in the drawer.

A few days later I took my freshly washed clothes to hang in the backyard. The neighbor's radio blared across to me: 'For God so loved the world, LOVED THE WORLD, that He gave His Son to die for my sins...for `your sins. His love is great. He forgave and lives in my heart.

Then the sweet-voiced man said, 'Come to Jesus. He loves you, too, and wants to give you peace, no matter what your circumstance. Kneel where you are and confess you sin and accept Jesus into your life.

I dropped to the dust beside the tree stump and cried out in sorrow for God to have mercy on me and to forgive my sin.

Two weeks later, Jose, my boisterous, unfaithful, drunken husband, listened to your program and yielded to Christ.

Mr. Rat was not the only problem we had to deal with during those days of radio ministry. Wednesday afternoon we left our toddler with a young man we had picked up from the street. (He had needed lots of love and help so we took him into our home for several weeks. His life seemed to be spectacularly transformed. He said he wanted to help us for being so good to him.) Darkness had settled over the neighborhood by the time we returned from the studio. As we parked the car we heard little Billy's screams. Yes, all alone! Our "transformed" friend had pried open the mission cash box in the desk, taken all the money, some of my husband's clothing, and gone away, unconcerned for our precious toddler!

In spite of that experience the radio broadcast went out the next Friday afternoon. Billy stayed with our missionary colleagues. In spite of a power failure, we prepared to proclaim the Gospel via the radio. We spent fifteen minutes praying for lights and current. The power returned just in time. In spite of another visit from Mr. Rat, we continued to sing.

Nothing was going to stop the program! It was intended to be "streams in the desert" for many dry lives.

## 28  BILL—IN A JAIL CELL? (1957)

"NAÏVE MISSIONARY SPENDS FOUR HOURS IN GUAYAQUIL JAIL!"–so reads the title on my journal page. I was trying to be funny.

Here's the story: A new believer from my English Bible class called and said, "I have a chocolate pie for you. Can Bill pick it up today?"

Bill hopped in the car and hurried away. It seems that a policeman in the middle of the street couldn't make up his mind. Bill thought he motioned him to stop and then to go on. Bill went on around the corner. But–the policeman whistled for him to stop. Then came the blow! Bill had been keeping his driver's license in the glove compartment because it was such a nuisance to keep changing it from shirt to shirt. Missionary men didn't keep important things in their pants pockets because of pickpockets. But this day he didn't realize he had taken the license up to the apartment and forgotten to return it to the car.

"You don't have your license?" asked the smug policeman. "Then on to jail."

Bill didn't fret, although the police only allowed him to phone the U.S. Consul. He sat on a musty old cot and talked for almost four hours to his cell mate, explaining about his personal faith in the Lord. The Consul spoke up for Bill and my husband was released, with the promise to appear the following morning at ten o'clock with the proper identification papers, including the license.

That morning the judge smiled at Bill, looked at his papers, shook his hand, and dismissed him. Without a fine! We were all praying that the fine would be small because our budget couldn't stand any strain right then. But, no fine at all was never considered! Bill ran from the car to our door and entered as only he can enter, quietly with his lopsided grin brightening his handsome face. He was grateful that the Lord had helped him in this dilemma.

We never did get the chocolate pie.

## 29 BLESSED ARE THE FLEXIBLE (1957)

"Blessed are the flexible, for they shall be stretched but not broken." I can't find that phrase in any book and I don't think it really is original with me! It is not in my Bible, either. I've taken it as one of the statements for my life's philosophy, though. The Lord has helped me to put that to the test, especially at Christmas time.

It was our second Christmas in Guayaquil. Bill and I had made a promise to God and to each other that we would make our Christmas Eve celebrations meaningful for people who would in no way have any of the "extras" for a special holiday observance. Christmas Eve is the real celebration in Ecuador, not the Christmas Day dinner.

We had an "interesting" tree that year. I had found an artistically formed branch out in the field, brought it to the house, painted it silver, and placed it in a silvered bucket. No pine trees were available back then. The red and blue balls looked almost exotic on that transformed desert branch. The delightfully decorated house looked great! A long plank table was set for twelve people and tantalizing aromas tickled our nostrils. I was tired and excited. We had invited nine people so two chickens were roasting in the oven. I hurried to the bedroom to change my clothes since it was almost nine o'clock, time for the guests to arrive. Who was coming? A janitor and his grandson, a shoe-shine fellow, a laundress and her children, and a trash collector. Bill came into the bedroom, flopped on the bed, but then sat up abruptly and gave me some disconcerting news. "Honey, I almost forgot to tell you. I invited the Ortega family to join us tonight. Alfonso is without work and they have absolutely nothing."

My response was surely not spiritual as my emotions hit a peak. I had a slipper in my hand. "How could you invite SEVEN more people? How can I stretch the food?"

I threw my slipper at my husband! He caught it. The only harm done was my attitude.

I almost fell apart. He said, "I'm not worried. There always seems to be room for one more!"

"But SEVEN more?"

There WAS enough food. To this day I'm not sure how the food stretched as far as it did. Add some more rice in the pot, more water and a few bouillon cubes to the soup. Not to mention I found some little gifts and wrapped them quickly and nervously. It all worked out beautifully. Bill and Billy were happy to help serve. We were happy, as it appeared were our guests. Blessed and happy are the flexible.

## 30 GOD INTERVENED (1958)

Bill and I were so glad to be serving people there in Ecuador, helping to start churches, teaching English to eager city students, taking care of visitors from far-away places, and participating in evangelistic campaigns. That is what God's love is all about.

One day I began to feel very strange. My legs cramped strangely, my body ached and seemed out of control, my neck felt tight, and my jaws hurt. These feelings increased until by sunset I was in intense pain, my body convulsing and my head jerking, my jaw getting more and more rigid.

"Go to the neighbor and tell her to call Daddy at the institute," I stammered almost incoherently to our pre-schooler. "What's happening?" I cried aloud. I couldn't pray. I couldn't shout for help. In my heart I pleaded, "Lord, take care of little Billy." I thought I was dying. Nobody could possibly live through these excruciating convulsions, these cramps, and this rigid sensation that something foreign wanted to possess my body.

In the hospital my husband heard the doctors say, "There is no anti-toxin here." In my coma Jesus held me in His arms. No other place was safe for me. As I "went out" I was only aware of being held securely with a bright, comforting light surrounding me.

Two days later my husband listened to the doctors discuss my case and conclude, "There is no way we can take the five-month fetus. It will kill her and the baby is already dead."

The convulsions had strangled the baby I carried.

While I lay like someone who was dead for several days, God was intervening. Before we had left for South America several people had promised to "cover us" with regular, specific prayer. That was very encouraging to us. One of those persons was my very own mother in Cleveland, Ohio. The night Bill rushed me to the hospital with my jaw locked and my body in convulsions, Mom received a strong impression in her heart to pray for me. She assumed that I was in trouble because of the previous miscarriage during my last pregnancy. She alerted two prayer partners. So Alpha, Irene and my mother were on their knees before the sofa the next morning, praying with strong supplications for me when the news came: "Lois gravely ill—TETANUS—only God."

My sensitive younger sister, Barbara received the call. She has given me her journal to copy from:

> Lois has more vitality and fun in her than any ten people I know…and people love her. She has always been the closest and dearest person and friend to me. I have gone to her with problems and joys never even uttered to another soul. And she has helped me. I can remember when she used to take me to the public library and then read fairy tales to me in the sunshine in the park by the lake.
>
> Lois contributed much to my being what I am. She taught me to love God and to love culture, to appreciate other good things of life—music, art, books. I admire her greatly.
>
> After she went to Ecuador I missed her terribly, but I gradually got over it. During those years, that she was gone, no one else had taken her place in my heart. Lois was in her fifth pregnancy, happy because she had Billy. But that baby didn't live because of something that happened.
>
> It was in the summer. I received the phone call with the cable that told about a very serious disease, tetanus. All of us knew that this dreaded thing was commonly fatal. Those weeks were a nightmare. We all knew it would be hard to get the right medical attention in that dirty city of Guayaquil!

I got into the habit of crying myself to sleep. It was not unusual to see red eyes in the rest of the family members' faces. We prayed as never before.

A plane, readied to leave Panama with the anti-toxin was prevented from taking off for forty-eight hours because of vicious storms! God held me in His arms.

"I'll serve as private nurse for Lois until someone else can take over," Baptist missionary Georgia Teel volunteered, even though she had two small children at home. Grethe Andersen, a nurse from Denmark, waiting to leave the U.S., received her visa for Ecuador from the Chicago Consulate and arrived in Guayaquil just as Georgia nearly fainted and stumbled out of the hospital due to extreme fatigue.

HCJB, missionary short wave radio station in Quito, beamed out the urgent word. People who didn't even know me prayed for me. Elisabeth in New Zealand wrote, "I have faith that God has yet a job for you. I'm praying." Another in Texas sent a postcard "Take courage, child of God. We are all praying." All around the world dozens more responded to the plea for prayer.

GOD INTERVENED. The activity of PRAYER had brought a miracle. Maria and Angelica of the downtown church stayed in the hospital corridor for hours on end, in prayer vigil. God brought me out of tetanus. Even though the baby was dead, no infection set in. God held me secure in His care. I became aware of a soft, accented voice reading from Hebrews, chapter four, minutes before I was able to lift a finger or speak a word as I came out of the coma. Grethe was reading the Bible aloud for me.

The neurologist and obstetrician stood at attention beside the door when I left the hospital. I smiled weakly with all the gratitude of my shining heart. Their smiles were shining, too, when one said for all to hear, "There goes our walking miracle."

My thoughts raced to respond, "Oh no, I am not YOUR miracle. I am GOD'S miracle!"

Now as I look back, I wish I had had the strength to SHOUT it outloud!

The missionary family lovingly cared for "my men". Edna Sparrow supplied hugs, clean clothes, good-night kisses, and chocolate cake for my precious son. Oh, God has blessed us in so many ways. Because He spared my life I have even more grateful incentive to obey Him and demonstrate His love.

# 31 A DANCE IN THE STREET (1960)

While Edna Sparrow was in the U.S. for their year's homeland ministry, I was given the treasurer/bookkeeper responsibility. I am thankful that when she returned she was very patient and understanding about the mistakes I had made.

One day I left the bank, clutching very tightly the small zipper case filled with money. Just as I turned down our street, a man ran up to me and grabbed at the bag. I held on with both hands so tenaciously that he swung me around—and around—and around. He swore at me. I held my balance and refused to let go. But, as you can imagine, I was just as frightened as I was determined!

We danced around there in the street but I kept a tight grasp on the mission's money!

Finally he let out an ugly expletive, released his hold on the bag and ran off. I trembled.

For a few seconds I couldn't move. Later, as I thought about that experience I thanked God that the man didn't kick or stab me. That seemed strange. I'm sure God's angel prevented him!

I walked with quaking knees to the mission compound. Bill and two pastors were praying as I literally burst into the room. "Gracias a Dios; aqui tengo todos los sucres." Or "Thank the Lord, I have all the money here." One sucre then equaled five U.S. cents. The case contained the equivalent of $1,200.00 U.S. I was filled with horror that I had almost lost it.

After I related the incident and took a couple of aspirins I felt better. After that day we went to the bank in the car.

# 32  MIGUEL SAID, "I BEAT MY BACK UNTIL IT BLED" (1961)

A crowded bus snaked its way over the graveled road from Quito, the capitol of Ecuador, to the port city of Guayaquil. It was a gray morning, the first rays of the sun had not yet touched the surrounding snow-capped peaks. A timid young fellow dressed in heavy wool pants and a worn jacket occupied one of the back seats. His cheeks were ruddy, his eyes clouded. From time to time he slumped down, head in his hands.

His name was Miguel. He had been told that in Guayaquil he would find the missionaries who could explain many things about the Bible. As the countryside slipped by, Miguel thought back over the years. One-by-one, images crowded onto the screen of his memory. He remembered his childhood with a fanatically religious mother, the many hours spent on his knees before statues and burning candles, and most vividly, his entrance into the monastery.

In the monastery Miguel began a serious life of unquestioning obedience, rigid discipline, and quiet meditation. Hours of repetitious prayer, chants, self-deprivation, and inner examination were all part of the monastic life. Explicit obedience to even the most illogical order was demanded. With a bitter smile he remembered one assignment—to plant an area of the garden with flowers put in upside down, the roots in the sunshine and the blossoms in the moist earth!

"I wanted to know the assurance that my sins were forgiven and have relief from the guilt I felt so deeply. I beat my back until it bled in order to call the attention of God to my repentance," Miguel revealed to us. One time he fell to the floor, semiconscious, his raw back a testimony to the intensity of his quest for pardon and peace.

Since Miguel was named monastery librarian he had access to the books during odd hours—his one, rare pleasure. One day he cautiously approached the shelves marked "prohibited." Surreptitiously he opened the forbidden books. What he read in those hurried moments ignited within him a spark of hope.

Then there was a radio receiver that he made from a match box—a crude little instrument with wires and earphones. It provided a solitary link with the outside world. And for Miguel, this insignificant-looking diversion became an instrument of blessing.

One morning, about 4:30 a.m., he caught faint strains for a few minutes. Then there was a clear phrase of gospel music. A hymn of supplication was followed by a message that left an indelible imprint on the young man's mind.

Miguel began to long for a better way of faith. He wondered about remaining in the monastery. He wanted to learn more about the Bible. Here are his own words regarding that momentous decision:

> Full of anxiety, I passed a seemingly unending night waiting for daybreak in order to flee. I was going away from that which had become a prison for me. The last hour had arrived in the cell where for ten continuous years I had served. Three o'clock! In the darkness I gathered a few small things (I didn't have much) and hastened to leave. I was determined that no one should stop me.
>
> Everything was quiet. All the monks were sleeping. The only thing that could be heard was the yowling of the early-prowling cats. Inside of me contradictions still stirred. But I had decided to leave—no steps backward!
>
> The solitary lamp of the main altar burned dimly, but by its faint light I easily found the door. The chilly wind of the Cayambe mountain whipped my body and, combined with fear, gave me a sensation like the terror of death.
>
> For the last time, I turned to look at the window of my cell. Those bars recalled many desperate struggles to reach pardon for my sinfulness.

Nothing had worked—not fastings, not disciplines of blood, nor entire nights of prayer on the cold cement floor. I was not certain what the future held when I left that chilly October morning.

I made my way over the rocky slope down toward the bus stop. I thought of all my companions. I knew them as evil. We lived together. I heard them talk. I knew their problems with sin, their injustice, their vices. I preferred the liberty of a vagabond to the hypocrisy of the pharisaical friars. I caught the bus to the center of the city.

In Quito, Miguel soon acquired a position as a teacher and there he found himself confronted with discrepancies in the religious philosophy he had studied. He developed friendships with Protestants. He later said, "I was surprised that I made friends with heretics!"

Because of social pressures and family conflicts, Miguel sought advice from a missionary in Quito who advised him to go to Guayaquil. Thus, it was that one Saturday morning our doorbell rang. When Bill opened the door, he saw only a sad-looking fellow in a jacket.

God saw a searching soul!

What joy for Bill and Stewart Sparrow to guide Miguel into a personal relationship with Jesus Christ, an assurance of forgiveness and a hope of heaven! Miguel said about that encounter, "I became a learner of the Word of God. I wanted to obey the admonition to Timothy to 'study to show myself approved by God, rightly dividing the Word of Truth' and be faithful to my newfound Saviour."

At this writing, Miguel is a Bible professor and pastor in Quito. Bill and I are blessed by the continuing friendship of Miguel and his wife, Nelly. Our son, Bill, has continued that friendship to this day.

# 33 WHAT HAPPENED TO THE CANDLESTICK? (1961)

Even in Ecuador where nice candles were usually impossible to find, I displayed the three heavy, very heavy glass heirloom candlesticks that Bill had inherited from Grandmother Miller. Often I put simple white candles from the open market in them. One afternoon, Grandmother's candlesticks, arranged on the table beside the sofa, beautifully reflected the sun. Fresh flowers on the coffee table and on the dining table brightened the area. I was ready for dinner guests who would come that evening.

Billy and Alvaro, our son's pal, sat on Billy's bedroom floor, playing with matchbox cars. I threw them a kiss and warned them, "Now don't go into the living room to play. It's all ready for tonight's special dinner. See you later."

When I returned from the women's Bible class I found two unusually quiet, angelic boys sitting on the back step coloring. How pleasant! Leaving my purse and Bible on the bed, I hastened to the kitchen, washed my hands, put on my apron, peeled the potatoes and lifted the lid of the garbage pail. My right hand, holding the peelings, halted in mid-air. What were those strange pieces of glass? I picked up a jagged triangle and muttered to myself, "This sure looks like that candlestick from Grandmother."

"Bill-ee-ee!" I shrieked. He came running. His guilty expression declared it all. Stammering and sighing, the boys owned up to their shenanigans. They had been bored. It was too hot to play ball on the grass outside, so, since the living room opened to a long hallway, one boy stood at the end of the sofa, directly looking into the hall. The other, at the end of the hall, threw the ball. But Billy's throw was too high. Alvaro missed the ball, hitting the candlestick which fell to the hard tile floor.

"Mom, I'm sorry. I really am. Hey, it's a good thing that only ONE of the candlesticks fell to the floor, isn't it?" I don't remember the punishment meted out that afternoon but I'm sure there was something. That night, when I tucked Billy into bed as usual with a song and a prayer, I realized with a very good feeling that I had not lamented the shattered candlestick. Oh, it was too bad…but it was only a THING. I was disappointed and indignant, not for losing the candlestick, but because our boy had disobeyed. How often must I give the Lord bad feelings because of MY disobedience?

# 34 A VICTIM OF THE MINERS (1961)

"I'm sorry, I don't feel free to leave our son with anyone right now. Bill can represent Ecuador in the Grand Junction conference. He doesn't need me." We three were in the U.S. for our year of deputation ministry.

"But, Lois, the church has asked for you and OMS wants to please the church. Couldn't you take the Greyhound and meet Bill there? He's in Texas right now, according to our schedule for him."

Three times I answered "No" to that request, but my mother exhorted me. "Lois, since they have asked so many times wouldn't that give you some indication that God really wants you out there? I'll be glad to care for Billy. He and little Bev (my sister, his aunt) get along beautifully."

The long, tedious trip with my feet propped up on a half bushel basket of apples to please the little old lady at my side left me with swollen legs and a very weary body. I stumbled off the bus in Colorado and said to the pastor, "Could I possibly lie down for awhile?"

Just as I was relaxing with my husband at my side, a gentle, but insistent knock summoned us to the door. "There's a couple at the church across the street who urgently need a Spanish speaking woman. Please go over with me."

With a sigh, I brushed my hair, put on my shoes, and took my Spanish Bible from the suitcase which I had packed not knowing I would need it, and walked across to the church. A couple was waiting for us. His hair was tousled and his clothing disheveled. He looked very anxious. His arm embraced an angry-looking woman whose brown-black eyes almost spit out her rage. The pastor said, "Here is Alex, a Russian who works up in the silver mine. Carmen is his Mexican wife. She speaks no English. He has told me their story briefly. Three times Carmen has tried to take her own life. Whenever he is gone from the house, the men in the camp come and force Carmen into a sexual experience. She is tired of being abused."

"Les odio…no valgo nada…les odio…les odio." (I hate them, I'm worth nothing, I hate them, I hate them.)

Bill accompanied Alex into the pastor's study and I took Carmen by the hand into the library. Right away I knew why I had endured the unpleasant bus ride. Carmen needed the Lord! With my Spanish I could talk with her and lead her to Christ. But whenever I mentioned the name of Jesus she trembled all over and hugged her arms to her chest. "Oh, Lord, give me wisdom, have mercy." I prayed silently in my heart and continued to talk to her about God's love and the sacrifice of Jesus for her sins. She leaned over and exclaimed, "No! No! No!"

I knew something strange was going on. This woman was so possessed by hate she wouldn't allow me to get through to her heart. I got down on my knees and looked up into her contorted face. She spit at me. I grabbed her arms. Then only God directed my words, "In the name of my powerful, sovereign Lord Jesus I say, 'go away from Carmen, whoever you are, go away from her. Leave her alone, in the name of Jesus, in the name of Jesus'!" I continued pronouncing the name of Jesus. Carmen went limp into my arms and began to weep. I cried with her.

"Carmen, ¿quieres orar? ¿Quieres ponerte en las manos de Cristo y aceptarle como tu Salvador personal?" (Carmen, do you want to pray? Do you want to put yourself in the hands of Christ and accept Him as your personal Savior?)

We went into the church sanctuary and knelt at the altar. Carmen was now quiet. Her broken phrases convinced me of her sincere repentance. At last, when Bill came into the sanctuary with the pastor and Alex, giving the news that Alex had been saved, Carmen could smile! God had transformed her, freeing her from the demons that drove her to hate and suicide. I thought of the hymn:
> *Glorious freedom! Wonderful freedom!*
> *No more in chains of sin I repine!*
> *Jesus, the glorious Emancipator*
> *Now and forever He shall be mine.*

# 35 I COULD SING! (1962)

Earl Smith, the pastor of our home church in Cleveland, was very solemn as he announced, "Lois has consulted with the doctors at the Cleveland Clinic about the growth in her throat and her inability to sing. They said that she needs surgery soon for the tumor on the thyroid. The X-ray has shown that it is against the vocal chords."

I obeyed God's Word (James 5:14-16) in asking the elders to anoint me and to pray for me. I'll always hold the picture in my memory of those beloved people showing their love for me that way.

Four days later Bill and I began packing to return to Ecuador. The previous day, I happily sang a solo in our farewell service. Since my voice had been restored, I thought God was healing me completely so Bill and I agreed to go ahead with our plan to end the furlough year on schedule.

Upon arrival in Guayaquil, we launched into all the challenges of evangelism. Yet, every time I bathed I was uneasy about the slight protrusion on the left side of my throat. I had no pain, no hoarseness, no discomfort. My friend advised me, "Go to SOLCA (The Cancer Research Institute of Guayaquil). The doctors there will know what to do.

A few days later the X-ray revealed that what showed as an obstruction of the vocal chords in the X-rays of Cleveland Clinic was now different. Nothing touched the vocal chords now! That's what had enabled me to be able to sing. The Ecuadorian surgeon gave an emphatic "yes" to the question of surgery so without hesitation, I checked into the hospital the following Wednesday. No problem resulted. The second Sunday following surgery, I stood in the Berea Church and sang praise to my God.

The whole experience was a stirring reminder that God's timing is perfect and that every episode of trust can present opportunity. During the four days of recuperation in the hospital the Lord blessed my witness of faith. A young nurse prayed to accept Jesus as her Savior. Now she can sing praise to her God as well!

# 36 YOU NEVER KNOW WHO'S WATCHING (1963)

My husband, our son Billy and I enjoyed one of the best vacations we've ever had down on the beach of Salinas, Ecuador. We rented a large room in a rustic old hotel and even took Billy's cat and her new-born kittens!

Our devotional hour on the beach just before sunset was the high point of the day. We almost always sat on some rocks in the same place with the waves lapping around our bare feet. We sang together (we did that so often), read a Bible portion, and then prayed together for fifteen consecutive days.

Back at home in Guayaquil those experiences were pleasant memories. Then, on a Sunday afternoon, our doorbell rang. There stood a handsome young couple who hesitantly inquired, "Is this where the American couple with the little boy live?"

"We're the Millers and Billy is our son," we replied. "Come in. What can we do for you?"

The young woman blurted out, "You can tell us about those little meetings you three had every afternoon on the beach in Salinas!"

The man continued, "We sat on our porch every late afternoon and watched you arrive at the rocks. We wondered what you were doing because we heard your singing. So we 'sneaked up' on you once and heard the three of you singing about Jesus Christ. Now we've come for you to explain that. We asked all around and finally found you."

Bill answered their questions with the Bible, explaining our personal faith. Dusk came and we had to stop the conversation for Bill to preach in the Bible Center Church. The young man, Federico, and his attractive wife began to read the Bible and attend the services in the Bible Center Church. Another Sunday afternoon, in our living room, the dialogue over the Scriptures resulted in their repentance and acceptance of Christ as Savior. Federico had studied Marketing and Economics in the university and was prepared for the business world, but God intervened and changed his plans. He answered the Lord's call to preach the Gospel.

Our seemingly insignificant daily devotions on the beach had opened the door to their obedience to the Lord. We never know who is observing us every day!

# 37 WE SEARCHED FOR TREASURES IN THE DARKNESS (1963)

Going to the back streets of hell was not our idea!

"Oh, Lois, I feel so embarrassed and tense."

"I know what you mean. All these men and boys milling around give me a weird feeling. And that raucous music only seems to accentuate the sordidness and darkness of their motives for being here."

I held tightly to Marta's arm as we walked down the dirt street. Closed doors told sad stories. Thousands, yes, I said "thousands" of women, all sizes, all ages, gaudily made up, their brief—sheaths leaving no room for modesty, hopefully lured their customers.

"This isn't the time, Lois. Let's get out of here now. We'll not find the French woman in this crowd."

"Yes, let's get back to the bus stop. We'll come in the morning. I was told that most of the women stay here all the time."

As I returned home on the city bus that afternoon, I mulled over the reasons that had brought us to the red light district. Miguel, a monasterial student converted to Christ, had shown up on our doorstep the previous Thursday morning.

"Dear sister Lois, I've been assigned six city blocks in the city visitation program."

"That's nice," I said, "To be a good pastor you'll have to have door-to-door experience like that."

"Oh, but you don't understand. Those blocks are where the men go to find prostitutes. I can't start there. Look at me. I'm so young. I'm scared, too. I wouldn't know how to tell those women about the Gospel."

"You poor fellow." I felt sorry that Miguel seemed so embarrassed. His brown eyes glistened with tears.

"Sister Lois, why don't you go out there and visit those women? You could find a companion from one of the churches."

"Oh, I don't think so Miguel. I don't think so. But my husband and I will pray that somebody will go in your place."

Now Marta and I were involved. We and my dear friend, Genoveva were the answer to that prayer! Betty Rehner joined the team later for awhile. Frenchie was one of our first targets of love. The newspaper vendor at the corner had teased us, saying, "Hah, why don't you go after Frenchie? She's surely about the hardest nut to crack—alcoholic, bitter, and she's been a prostitute since she left the ballet over twenty-five years ago."

All the women on the street were staring. Tongues wagged. "What are those women going to do?" As if responsible for the reply, the tag-along, ragged children said, "They're looking for Frenchie!"

"Huh?" piped up one woman. "Frenchie's asleep down around the corner in the doorway of the old shoe store."

We found her—all knotted up on the filthy dirt, feigning sleep. Marta and I looked at each other. "Should we wake her up?" Marta asked.

"No," I answered, "I'll write a little note and stick it in her dress neckline and she'll know at least that we've been looking for her."

Quickly I scribbled a note on the back of a gospel booklet and knelt to tuck it into Frenchie's dress. Fluttered eyelids revealed her wakefulness. Then, opening bloodshot eyes, Frenchie croaked, "You did come! I told them you'd find me."

News had traveled fast in the district and Frenchie knew we were looking for her! Curious onlookers multiplied and pressed around us three. I lifted Frenchie to her feet. She probably weighed all of ninety pounds. "Now, you just lean on me."

I darted a questioning look at Marta, as if to say, Where will we take her? Both of us lived on the far side of the city. Stopping in the shade of a mango tree, Marta prayed aloud. (She wanted Frenchie to know that we were spiritually concerned for her.) "Oh, dear Lord, thank you that we've found this little lost lamb. Thank you that you love Frenchie. Now guide us to a place of refuge for her. Amen."

Frenchie leaned hard on my shoulder and murmured, "Amen."

The five blocks to a believer's house seemed more like ten miles. Often Frenchie whimpered and at times raised her green eyes to mutter, "I love you."

She was so tiny. Even small Marta could have carried her. To quiet her whimpering I began to sing. When I stopped to catch my breath, Frenchie burst out, "Sing, keep singing. I like it. It makes me feel good."

What an eloquent picture we presented as Frenchie limped beside us, her right foot badly swollen from a fall while in a drunken stupor. Blood from an open sore on her leg stained Marta's skirt. Every two or three minutes she turned to the children crowding around us and growled, "Go away, you ugly ducklings. Go away!" But they kept on following behind, just like the Pied Piper of Hamlin tale.

At the believer's home Frenchie was settled in the hammock. I said, "Now promise to be a good girl, Frenchie, until I can come back with a nice dress for you."

And then Frenchie pleased us for she promised to attend the women's Bible class with us that afternoon.

And she did! This usually sullen, bitter alcoholic (who everyone in the district said would be the hardest case) responded to our love. She wore the simple cotton dress, her hair was combed neatly in place, and her face was scrubbed clean of the gooey make-up she usually wore. She seemed rational and attentive and sat up in the class like a royal lady.

(Later I learned that Frenchie [her real name was Georgina] had come from an aristocratic family in France. She had expected to dance in the large cities of Ecuador; but because of bad choices and alcohol, she fell in with manipulative men. Her evil pimp demanded much from Frenchie. She gave in and became a slave in the red light district.)

I took Frenchie to our house that night. How disturbed I was to find her in the middle of the night making a racket, tossing cans and bottles all around the kitchen, looking for an alcoholic drink, cursing in anger. She remained in our home four days, going into spasms, crying out in absolute agony because I would not give her any gin. That fourth afternoon, while I was outside the home, Frenchie ran—back to her bottle—back to the tragic life of her past years.

Genoveva, Marta, and I continued in the red light district, making fragile friendships with the suspicious women there. They were close-mouthed. No one would give any news of Frenchie.

A couple of weeks later, while I was entertaining some VIPs from our US office, a taxi stopped in front of the house. Frenchie appeared at the screen door of the living room, and with the stilted voice of a snobbish duchess she ordered, "You can pay my taxi."

She sailed into the room, naked except for her pink panties. She had sold her Bible, her dresses, and her shoes and drank until she was very, very drunk. And she confessed, "I took your pretty diamond ring, Lois. The man at the pawn shop didn't give me very much for it though."

I hustled her into bed as I would a naughty child, scolding her for her behavior. She smiled wanly and hugged me, whispering, "I love you lots. And I want to love God, I really do. Pray for me."

I had looked for my engagement ring and could not imagine what had happened to it. Frenchie and I went to the pawn shop the next morning and retrieved my ring. But Frenchie remained in her little cane shack.

Genoveva and I found Frenchie the next week when we entered her street. She was huddled in the doorway of the shoe store. Her disheveled hair had no shine in the sun and her dirty face was streaked with tears. We sang about God's grace to her, accompanied by the taunts and profanity of the women slouching nearby. I hugged my French treasure. We three women walked away—Genoveva and me with bodies erect, but with hearts bent low.

Frenchie again went to our home. That night, even though Billy had school the next day, he cooperated with us in making Frenchie quiet down. He sat on the back patio with his Bible, reading aloud to her. She whined, "Don't you stop now. No, not now. Keep on reading, little friend."

He resumed reading for about another hour from the Gospels. Frenchie blurted out to me the next morning, "Is it OK for me to tell God I'm sorry for being so bad and to ask for His forgiveness? Is it OK? Will Jesus be my Savior?"

The hard nut cracked before God's mercy and love. But the pitiful treasure of grace fell back again and again and again. The last time I talked with her (before leaving for ministry in the US) she smiled and said, "I'm mad at you for leaving; but if you don't come back here, I'll see you in heaven."

Miguel's plea for help resulted in several shining treasures to be taken from the darkness—

Hermenegilda, Frenchie's companion of 27 years, was baptized by Miguel and became the treasurer of the women's group in his church. She later married a very elderly man who left her with a lovely house and money to live comfortably when he died. Her daughter studied in the university and eventually became a medical doctor.

Filipina, whose pimp cut her hands with his razor because she listened to us tell about salvation, escaped very late one night. We took her back to her mother's house in the country.

Berta, whose slothful husband was responsible for her activity there, accepted the Lord in a women's Bible study group. Eventually her husband came along to the church, too.

While we were in the United States I received word that Frenchie's body had been found, curled up in newspaper on the cement of the entrance to a vacant store. She was buried in a pauper's grave.

# 38 DAVID'S SPECIAL VISITOR (1963)

David Campos, a radiant teenage osteomylitis victim, was feeling weak and very sad. He had not slept well in the hospital. One morning his father, Felipe, stopped to visit David on his way to work. David brightened up a bit when his father prayed, "We're trusting the Lord for His touch on you son," he said.

They reminded each other of David's older brother's words the week before to their mother, "Mamacita, I believe God is going to heal David. I know that I have to be faithful in praying for him because God has called David to preach. I'm not called, but I know how to pray."

Then Felipe said to David, lying so white and drawn on the bed. "Your little brother, Felipito, scolded the little ones yesterday afternoon. He said, 'Hey, kids, let's be more quiet. Mama has to pray for David. Come on, I've got an idea. Let's pray for David now.' So they made a circle of prayer for you my son."

Felipe left the hospital room. He looked up to wave from the street corner where he always waited for the bus. David's bed was beside the window. Felipe was startled. He saw a tall figure, dressed in white, standing beside his son's bed. The figure's hands were extended over the bed and his head was bowed. Felipe said to himself, "My, it's strange that don Guillermo (Bill) or don Alfredo (Alfredo Colom) would be visiting at 7:15 in the morning!"

Felipe blinked and looked again. The figure was still there, erect with head bowed. The father thought about that scene all day long. The first words he said to his wife, Ruth, later were, "Wife, you know I don't have much of an imagination! Wait 'til you hear what happened this morning at the hospital."

Ruth had not gone to visit their son that day. She listened with trembling attention to her husband's account. Then whispered, "Era el angel del Señor...o Jesus." (It was the Lord's angel or Jesus.)

Together they visited the next day. David had slept well all night without pain. He had eaten all the breakfast on the tray. He had not been aware of any special visitor the day before but he knew he felt better not only in his body but also in his spirit. One week later, David was sitting up, taking short walks and showing a smile. His doctor acknowledged God's touch when David declared, "This is of God! My brothers and sisters and the missionaries have been praying for me every day!"

David recovered well. Today he has only a slight limp which does not hinder his activity. He has a fruitful pastoral ministry with radio preaching and counseling in Guayaquil. We continue to appreciate our family's friendship with him to this day.

# 39 LASSIE CAME HOME! (1964)

Billy's "little sister", as he called her, was his loyal, beautiful English collie. We all appreciated her beauty as well as her obedience. For example, when a fellow missionary who always said that animals belong in the farmyard came to our door, Lassie would reluctantly, but obediently, take her place behind the sofa and be as quiet as a mouse. Or when we sat at the table she didn't beg for tidbits but lay beside Billy's chair, knowing that he'd slip her some goodies now and then.

Most of our neighbors lost their watchdogs to thieves who passed poisoned meat through the gate to the animals, waited for them to die, and then climbed over the wall to rob the home. Lassie delayed in learning this new lesson. She was not to touch any food without Billy's or my command. We weren't sure she had really learned that lesson until one Sunday when we returned from church. Billy unlocked the gate and Lassie came whining to him. There on the cement walk was a big hunk of meat. The flies buzzed around it but Lassie had evidently not touched it.

Soon after that incident Lassie disappeared. All that day the gates had been open because people were coming and going. Four NOW Corps (Novice Overseas Witnesses, usually second or third-year college students) were working on the patio, tutoring some of their Ecuadorian students in English. Billy came home from school that afternoon calling out as usual, "Lassie, Lassie girl, where are you?" No response came from Lassie.

Billy rode his bicycle all around the neighborhood, shouting out his dog's name. No one had seen her. By dinnertime he was very tired and overwhelmed by sadness. He had no appetite. When Bill excused him from the table he went to the screen door and lay down. "Mom," he said, "when you go to bed leave the gate open a little bit so Lassie can come in."

Bedtime came. The boy refused to sleep. He had to keep vigil. It was almost midnight, Ralph and Joanie, the young married NOW corps couple, were in their bedroom. Bill and I were lying on our bed, feeling Billy's emotion, unable to sleep. Only an occasional bird sound penetrated the quiet night. Then, all of a sudden, we heard a faint sound. We bounded to the window, Lassie was limping toward the front door. Billy threw himself at her, hugging her with all his strength. She licked his face and fell down with a groan. Bill and I ran to the door, almost colliding with Ralph and Joanie. We all fell down to pet Lassie. Her lovely coat was matted with blood, her mouth was lacerated and her legs were cut and bruised. Then I abruptly looked up at Joanie. She looked down at me and we both blushed. Our chiffon nightgowns were not very appropriate attire. Ralph's undershorts were only a bit better. Our commiseration with Lassie had to be interrupted while we went for our robes.

Lassie was a smart dog. I don't know how she got away from her captors. We were all just thrilled that Lassie had come home! We were a complete family again.

## 40 BILLY'S PASTOR-PARTNER (1964)

Enrique Guillen came to Guayaquil from the coastal town of Salango, about fourteen months after his conversion in order to study for the ministry. God had called him from the small town sustained by its coffee production and fishing industry. My husband loved this brother in the Lord, eight years younger than he, and encouraged him when he entered the third grade of the elementary school. Yes, I said "third grade". Imagine this mature man crowding his knobby knees under the student desk! In order for him to learn to read and write so that he could study for the ministry he had to go back to the regular classroom.

Even while he was working on his elementary school education, Enrique began to preach, using Bible texts that he aptly quoted from memory. One day I came upon Billy and Enrique in a contest to see who could quote more verses from memory!

In 1964, our disgruntled son complained one Sunday morning. "Oh, Dad, do I have to go to Sunday School? I'm bored. I know all the Bible stories. I really think I could tell them as well, maybe even better, than the teacher. Don't make me go."

Dad was gently adamant so Billy went. "We'll see what we can do about your problem, son," his dad reassured him.

Enrique, newly appointed as student-pastor to the Divine Redeemer Church, came each week along with two or three other novice pastors, to pray with Bill in the Church Association Office. Bill shared his concern about Billy's boredom with them. Enrique spoke up, "He could teach the children's class for us. He's bigger than the other children. They won't know he's so young. While he's there he can play the little pump organ for the service." That was our son's first church assignment. He and Enrique were pals—partners in ministry.

Upon completing his studies, Enrique assumed the pastorate of the church at the sugar mill. The church grew and even established several flourishing daughter churches. He was president of the Church Association for several years. At this writing, he is looked upon as a "patriarch of blessing". He is another one who is still in touch with Billy (Bill III) who still does joint ventures with Enrique when he takes missions trips to Ecuador.

# 41 GOD PROTECTS (1964)

If we could only see into the invisible world, we would be astounded by the amazing ways God protects us, through angels, through people we don't even know, even through circumstances He has maneuvered.

Young missionary women need prayer for protection because they are usually unaccustomed to the sensual attitude of the worldly men in most cities of our world. One morning, I stepped down off the bus at the riverside marketplace. I couldn't, however, move forward. I was blocked by the six or seven young men who closed in around me. The roguish gleam in their eyes and the words they spoke were disturbing to say the least. One said, "Now, sweet thing, just step over behind that wall and we'll have some fun." Another said, chuckling, "Oh, yes, we like women with your rounded out figure."

I looked from face to face and began to tremble. Then the Holy Spirit surged within me. I declared, however shakily, "En el nombre de Jesucristo les mando que abran este circulo." (In the name of Jesus Christ, I demand that you open this circle.)

One smirked, "Ha, she's an evangelical." To my relief, they sauntered away laughing amongst themselves.

---

Another time, when Marta and I were visiting the women of the red light district, I stayed too long talking to Felipa. Marta had already gone home. There were no buses for me. At the corner, I hailed a taxi. No doubt he wondered about the foreign woman at the corner of "prostitute row," now that the sun had set and it was dark.

I told him to take me to Urdesa, Calle Primera where I lived. Bill was out of town with an Every Creature Crusade team. Billy was at home with our live-in helper. I settled back and closed my weary eyes. When I opened them we were NOT going in the direction of Urdesa, but in the opposite way—out to the darkness of the streets along the estuary. I swallowed hard, took a deep breath, and croaked: "Where are you taking me? Turn around and take me to Urdesa." The man only chuckled in response.

I screamed, "In the name of my Savior Jesus Christ I demand that you take me back to the pavement. I'll get another taxi. Turn around in the name of the Lord!"

He slammed on the brakes, turned around to me and said, "You're an evangelical believer?" I nodded my head. "OK, señora, I'm sorry."

I wanted to get out right there but there was no bus or any taxis in sight. I slumped down on the seat with tears rising to the surface. My heart pounded. The man drove carefully back to the pavement and took me home. He accepted my payment along with a tract without saying another word. With tears on my pillow that night I expressed my gratitude to the Lord for His protection.

## 42 GOD ALERTED HIS ANGELS (1965)

Two or three times each week Genoveva, my Ecuadorian partner, and I went out to the red light district to demonstrate God's love through personal witness. Over 4,000 prostitutes worked in that huge port city of Guayaquil. One morning in July, we stepped down off the bus at the corner. We were ready to love the women through bologna sandwiches, listening ears, and prayer. We approached the red door of Leopoldina, well-known for her caustic tongue. She listened rather well that day while we stood at the door of her split-cane shack, but she didn't respond. Just as we were leaving her, two swarthy, drunken men lurched towards us from the corner.

"I'll take the full-figured one (me) and you can grab the skinny one." Empty shacks with doors ajar were available to these men on each side of Leopoldina's shack. My heart jumped to my throat. Genoveva began to tremble. I was so frightened I couldn't move. I couldn't think. I couldn't speak. Leopoldina cackled hoarsely and shut her door.

The man who had spoken grabbed the shoulder of my cotton dress. I was helpless with fear. Immediately his companion stumbled backward, looking behind us. "Vámanos de aquí," he exclaimed. (Let's get out of here.)

What was happening? The men looked behind us as they staggered back around the corner. Genoveva and I turned around. Two tall, uniformed guards stood there, at attention. My partner said in a barely audible voice, "What are you two doing here?" During almost three years of visiting the red light district during the daytime, we had never, NEVER seen a guard, a city policeman, a soldier, or a security person.

They touched their caps and one replied, "To serve you ladies. We followed you from the bus stop."

They turned and disappeared around the corner behind us. Genoveva and I hugged each other in relief and went to our homes. We had no strength to continue that morning. We had just escaped being raped! We were convinced in our hearts that those uniformed angels had been sent there to protect us!

Twelve days later, an airmail form from Greenville, Ohio appeared in our box. Peg Sneary, the writer, was one of a host of people who had promised to be prayer partners for us in the ministry to the prostitutes.

She wrote, "I was gathering the eggs on the morning of July sixth and had a strong impression to pray for you. The inner voice urged me to hurry. I went into the house and obediently prayed for your protection and well being. Did anything happen that day?"

She "dialed" heaven and placed her call to God through her INTERCESSION. God received her call. He promises to protect His own. He alerted His angels and they appeared. Because that prayer partner in Ohio was obedient in prayer, Genoveva and I were delivered. We never saw those angels again. We never saw any other uniformed guards again either. No doubt those angels were there though. We just didn't "see" them.

# 43  THEY WANTED A CATASTROPHIC TAKE-OVER (1966)

We had no idea that the young people would be threatened by a band of Communists when Billy was chosen by his high school to carry a floral wreath to place at the statue in the park on a special holiday. We parents, friends, and bystanders lined the main street and waited and waited and waited, wondering why the procession was delayed. We heard angry shouts and some heavy metallic thuds nearby. Finally, the band marched out onto the avenue, followed by the American School students. Billy's face was white. All the young people looked tense and strained. Later we learned that the young people were detained by a group of Communists who pushed market carts in their path, taking machine guns and clubs from the covered carts. Thankfully, someone had leaked the threat to the city police and to the military as well. Out from behind the pillars of the buildings and the parked cars flooded the brave and watchful policemen who put an instant stop to the intended violence.

During those years our beloved Ecuador was under spasmodic threat of a catastrophic take over of the government. The Communists were anxious to see their philosophy take hold, especially in the university and the outlying farming areas.

Our friend Pepe and his friends out near Hacienda Diosilda were flattered by the attention of the Communists who cleverly presented their tirades. As he worked, Pepe's machete hissed as it cut through the dry weeds. Perspiration trickled in dirty rivulets down his bare back to his trousers, which were secured by a rope belt. Ragged cuffs rubbed against his mud-splattered ankles, for he crossed the river often. His hair, cut "bowl style," was as black as carbon and his eyes darker than midnight, flashed as he looked out over his world. He worked very hard to achieve a meager existence by growing cacao, coffee, and papaya. As he worked, he repeated the Communists' phrases in his mind: "Your farms are too small. Your school is inadequate and antiquated. So called democracy is making your children naïve and your women more and more independent."

Pepe and his friends listened closely to their statements. "The rich are pocketing all the gains from the poor; the government is very corrupt, foreign religious leaders and missionaries are allowed to deceive your people. Most of all," they added, "the United States is making plans to take over Latin America!"

Pepe believed them. After all he reasoned, the Communist men were better educated, wore nicer clothing, and had grown up in his own country. They really wanted to raise the level of living, he thought. God used my husband and his Crusade team to persistently witness to Pepe and his friends. God changed their philosophy and their way of looking at things. He persuaded them of the Truth in Christ Jesus who is the Truth, the Life, and the Way! They began to recognize the error in what they were being told.

During those very days, Bill and I were developing a friendship with a professor of mathematics from Spain and his attractive Catalan wife who had attended the English classes of the Night Cultural Institute. He and his wife were sophisticated and well-educated although with a social pretension apparently designed to impress us. We still have the luxurious leather-bound copy of Don Quixote they gave us for Christmas. However, through a series of woeful disappointments, they were unmasked before us. At that time of unmasking Dr. Mena spouted out, "Just you wait. My cohorts and I will make you all suffer. I'll just let you know, Millers, that you're near the top of my list of evangelicals to be annihilated!" Evidently Miguel Lecaro, pastor of the largest church at that time, was at the top of the list, followed by the Christian layman who had instigated the investigation against Dr. Mena.

God took charge and they were eventually banished from Ecuador.

## 44 SHARED VICTORIES (1966)

Billy and I eagerly looked forward to the times my husband returned from the scenes of the Every Creature Crusades. One day, as Bill flopped down on the sofa, we wouldn't let him nap. We insisted he tell us the latest news about Quevedo. Those Crusades were a significant part of our lives because our prayers covered those endeavors.

"Well," Bill began, "Did you know that the kids call me 'the man who's going to take them to heaven?' Little Miguel blurted that out one day as I walked into the children's Bible club. They call me that because I had explained to them that Jesus is the Way to Glory."

He went on to tell us that bronze-faced Miguel was one of several who had accepted Jesus out of the one hundred children in the club, that a ninety-year-old grandmother was the first adult woman to be converted, that a deformed cripple was the first male convert. Probably the most outstanding conversion during those first days was a young father "arrested" by the Holy Spirit. Thirty dollars was burning his pocket. His employer had given him that extra money to cover the expenses of clinic, clothing, and medicine for his wife who was ready to give birth. His inclination, however, led him to go toward the street of the prostitutes. He passed the Crusade meeting on the way there. His wife was glad not only for the financial help because he did not spend it as he intended, but she was also glad for the change Jesus made in her husband's heart.

God made a change in the life of a woman who listened raptly to the Gospel during that time. The flames of a bonfire, built to burn her religious relics, statues, and pictures, licked the sky, lighting the form of her husband returning from a business trip. When she saw him approaching she trembled with fear. She was sure he'd rant and rave about the money he'd spent for those items. The Crusaders drew close to reassure her. The husband raised his voice, only to say, "I see you're doing some housecleaning." Later, he also joined the group of believers preparing for baptism.

Every time Bill shared such stories with us, we felt that we had a part in the victories and thanked the Lord. That has always happened with us—when I have a victory, Bill has a part in it, when he has a victory, I have a part in it. For God has joined us together to be "helpmates", "shareholders", and "partners" in ministry. In the same way, those of you who support us in prayer also share in each victory on the field. In a spiritual sense, YOU are there with us as we minister and you share in the fruit of those labors as well.

## 45  "CAST YOUR BREAD UPON THE WATERS…" (1970)

When we first moved into the apartment in Cuenca in 1970, the woman downstairs installed a shrine in her sewing nook where we could look down on it daily from our dining room. The satin-sequined figure of baby Jesus reclined in a fancy cradle surrounded by three bouquets of fresh flowers. The picture of the weeping Virgin hung behind it. A forty-watt bulb was placed just above the picture, illuminating it day and night.

Aida, my downstairs neighbor, was only thirty years old. She was reluctant to respond to our gestures of friendship. Oatmeal cookies one week, banana bread another day, cinnamon rolls and candy at Christmas, helped to break the resistance. I took time to color pictures with her children and taught them to make tissue paper stars and colored chains.

The first victory was Aida's accepting an invitation to an afternoon cup of coffee. A couple of months later, she accepted my invitation to the women's Bible study in our home. She attended spasmodically for a whole year before becoming a regular attender, but always sat very close to the door! She often lingered to chat with me though.

One night, after the children were asleep and her husband, a sixty-two-year old retired army captain, had left on a trip, she tiptoed upstairs and we read the fourteenth chapter of John together. She revealed many of her fears and prejudices as well as the sad details of her motherless childhood and unsatisfactory marriage. A couple of hours later I prayed with her and she kissed me goodnight.

Another victory came when Cuenca and the surrounding area was shaken by an earthquake at midnight. Aida shouted up immediately, "Señora Loida, come down and pray with me."

Vinicio, her second child, was mentally slow and emotionally disturbed. A few words here, a few sympathetic phrases there, and much prayer resulted in Aida's finally recognizing her son's need. I made the appointment with the psychologist and even accompanied them there. Vinicio was scared. So was his mother! When the doctor requested that the captain see him, we met resistance. So we prayed. Bill invited him for coffee. He had previously refused four invitations to our home. This time, the captain came. He opened up to Bill in a very sincere way, with the result that Bill went with him to the psychologist's office.

I began to notice that the flowers of the shrine were left to dry and droop. Sometimes the light was not burning. Aida purchased a New Testament and began reading the portions I suggested each night. Her faith became less form and more deeply spiritual.

Vinicio needed an operation. Aida asked me to accompany her. While her son was in surgery, she and I talked, prayed, and held hands. Aida was usually very nervous. Yet during Vinicio's recovery she allowed God to meet her need. She was calm without using pills!

During Holy Week the church had special evangelistic meetings. Aida, the captain, and the three children came a few times. At the Bible study the next week, Aida publicly stated her joy in systematically reading the Bible. She took notes very faithfully despite the fact that she felt she could never change her religion. What mattered most was that by that time, she had established a relationship with God that she never had before.

When Bill and I returned to Ecuador in May of 1998 to research and do interviews for a book in progress, I was surprised by a phone call our last night in Cuenca. I recognized Aida's unique voice immediately. She told us that she remembered us every week and was grateful to us and to God for our patience with her and our love for her.

She told us that the copious notes she took at the Bible studies were read and reread after we left Cuenca as she continued to read the Bible. She was sad, missing us. Then she said, "One day, it seemed that God was speaking to me through those notes. I told Him that I would follow the

Lord Jesus with my whole heart. My husband forbade my attendance at your church, so I went to Pastor Roberto and he said that I would be wise, for the moment, to conform to my husband's wishes. But I was so anxious to share all that I had learned from you and what God was teaching me through my Bible reading, that I invited a couple of friends to my house to share with them what I had learned. After a few months more came. Know what? I've kept up the class all these years that you've been gone. Now we have between thirty-five and thirty-eight women each week! All thanks to God and to you!"

## 46  HAIL, HAIL…THE GANG'S ALL HERE! (1970)

At two o'clock in the afternoon of October 3$^{rd}$, the electricians arrived with all their paraphernalia to put in 220 volt cables. But the weather wasn't cooperating! At that time, we had a special friend, an Ecuadorian teacher by the name of Enoe, who lived with us. Just as they dumped their stuff at the door of Enoe's room, where the wires were, our ears were bombarded with the loud pelting of hailstones. The men started their hammers.

Lassie started to whine. I paid no attention to her because my four English students arrived and bounced into the dining room. I gave them their exam and rushed to the pantry. Lassie, pawing and scratching at the screening on the rabbit's hutch, was angry. She had succeeded in ripping part of the door and poor Funny Bunny was huddled back in the corner. This added to the din of the storm and the workmen. I settled that problem. The hutch was put high up on the cupboard and Lassie received a harsh scolding.

"Oh, look, señora Loida, water's dripping from the ceiling! Now it's coming in over the bookcase. And look over there…!" Evidently the hailstones had cracked some of the tiles of the roof. We rushed to get the rug out of the way. We moved the books and brought things in to collect the incessant dripping ending up with seven pans and bowls in the living room, five in the hallway, and two in the dining room!

The men working in Enoe's room carried the cement through the hallway, their shoes dirty with cement dust. Two more men arrived from the Electric Company and proceeded to take down two rows of ceiling tile in the hallway. The water dripped heavily. "Oh, what's the use?" I said.

"We'll clean up when they're all through. The straw matrug is already ruined."

Where was Bill? Where was Billy? I felt alone with this disaster on my hands. The heavy Cuenca wool curtains were wet, the divan pillows were soggy, and the hail broke two panes of window glass in the office. The students laughed as they tried to help with rags and brushes to set things in order before they left.

Finally, Bill, Billy, Enoe and I illustrated what teamwork really is. Dusk came upon us as the electricians left, leaving behind wet plaster, cement kernels, and mud. We cleaned up the mess together. I had no more big pans or bowls left in the kitchen. All were catching drips! I felt like crying! Bill began to sing, "Y si todos trabajamos, unidos, unidos." (If we all work together, together.) Enoe and I giggled. Billy slid across the wet board floors on the rags, joining in with harmony to his Dad's song.

Enoe disappeared for a moment and then came rushing into the living room where I was on my hands and knees, dirty, disheveled, perspiring and sighing. She burst forth with, "Loida, the Baptist missionaries have come to give us a welcome. Hurry. You must greet them at the door."

I raised my head in disbelief! How could it be? I looked around the room. No cushions on the chair, no rug; the whole place wet and ugly. I stood, determined somehow to get through this, my mind racing, thinking that I had nothing to serve them except some fruit.

Enoe's eyes twinkled, "Joke…it's a joke, Loida. I just wanted to test your flexibility."

"Well, just for that, Enoe dear, you can go to the kitchen and make some sandwiches. We've got to eat something before the Bible study tonight."

I remember that a fellow missionary told me that in the missionary survival kit, it is necessary that there be a generous supply of humor. By the end of the ordeal, we laughed heartily together. I guess he was right!

# 47 "LITTLE LOCO" (1971)

Bill came back to the house from visitation late one morning with a strange six-year-old boy hanging onto his arm. I had heard about this neighborhood problem whose name was Medardo, but as a result of our loving attention that first time to our house, he became a frequent visitor and an emotional part of our lives. That first day he was drunk and belligerent, but quickly settled down on my lap as I sang lullabies and children's choruses to him.

The neighborhood children rejected him. He was bright and alert at times, terribly violent and unpredictable other times. Because of his despicable temper, the children shouted, "Loco, loco" (crazy, crazy) when he approached.

He usually came to our house at odd hours. When he came with an expression of terror because of hallucinations, I held him close and prayed. Then, Medardo usually fell asleep. One day I was giving instruction to a new Christian. Medardo marched in and demanded a cookie! I gave him the Snickerdoodle cookie, a sheaf of paper, and crayons. He sat down at the children's table near the kitchen door and began to scrawl using only the black crayon. He covered the paper, then the table, then the chair, and then up the wall. When I scolded him he spat out filthy, obscene words and phrases, ending with "I hate you, hate you, hate you!"

The next afternoon he perched on a stool in the kitchen. Suddenly his screams shattered the silence. "Oh, Mrs. Lois, the devil's coming. I can smell him! I'm scared." Immediately I grabbed him and called aloud to Jesus. I assured him, "The Lord Jesus has control in this house, Medardo."

Several times we had to replace roofing tiles because little "loco" walked on the roof. One Tuesday, he jumped to the street below and only dislocated an elbow although we lived on the second floor. He boasted about that feat!

Medardo, the second youngest of thirteen children, was often chained in the outer patio because his frantic mother, at her wits end, couldn't control him. His brothers and sisters harassed him. He said to me several times, "You're the only one who hugs me."

One afternoon, just as I finished arranging an elaborate buffet supper for a group of visitors from the States, Medardo knocked on our door. "Hey, let me eat some of that stuff on the table! It looks pretty."

"Come back tomorrow afternoon and I'll tell you a nice story."

"No, no!"

He reeked of whiskey. I didn't let him dig a spoon into the salads on the table, so he jumped up on me, his legs clamped around my waist. "I hate you, I hate you," His fingers clutched my throat as he hissed, "I'll kill you, kill you, kill you."

I tried to loosen his grip. His fingers pressed tighter and tighter on my throat. I got the door open and stumbled down the stairs, Medardo's legs tightening around my middle. We reached the street floor and I managed to croak out the words, "In Jesus' name, let me go, let me go, in Jesus' name." Just then Medardo's older brother came around the corner and forcefully took the boy who then slumped limply into his arms. My throat was sore and my voice was raspy for a couple of days.

At the next visit he gloated, "Aha, you can't control me. I go where I want to, do what I want to, say what I want to and nobody, NOBODY, can hold me down. What do you say to that?"

"I say, little friend, that Jesus Christ can get hold of your heart and manage you. Because the Lord Jesus is stronger than that whiskey you drink and more powerful than your boasts."

He looked at me questioningly, came over to my chair, climbed up on my lap and said, "Sing, sing, sing to me."

Other experiences with Medardo increased our concern for him. One day his brother came looking for him. He was nowhere to be found.

Late that afternoon some pilots appeared on the family's doorstep with Medardo in a drunken stupor. He had stowed away in the tail compartment of their little plane which was soon to be headed for the jungle.

One Wednesday evening, Medardo came into the little church during the prayer time and rushed to the piano to pound hard on the keys. I grabbed him and held him tightly. Finally, he relaxed his squirming and kicking and fell asleep. At the close of the prayer service, the five young men who were learning about prayer gathered around me. With a deep burden they gave Medardo a beautiful gift, they prayed for him with faith, laying their hands on his head and in the strong name of the Lord, asked Jesus to touch and protect the little boy. Medardo slept on. We all marched out together, carrying Medardo home.

Eventually the children stopped calling him "loco". After persistent, loving instruction, Medardo was able to study and settled into a Sunday School class, always a bit inquieto (restless).

Sometimes one has to experience the pain and perplexity of loving, in the obedient day to day attention to others! The experiences with Medardo softened our hearts to be prompted in a new way to love the little lost, even "loco" ones.

# 48 IT WAS UNBELIEVABLE! (1971)

I was all ready to entertain the Men for Missions Crusade team soon to arrive. The buffet table looked like it belonged on a cruise ship. The wooden stairs that led up from the street to the missionary apartment were scrubbed spotless. Bill planned to go to the airport for the visitors and just as I was putting the finishing touches to my hair, he decided to go down and wait for me in the van. He bounded down the stairs then hollered up to me, "Lois, come on down here. You'll never believe this!"

I grabbed my purse, rushed down the stairs, stopping abruptly as I hit the bottom step. What I saw was just as Bill had shouted. It was unbelievable! Who had done this repugnant thing? A pile of runny bowel movement lay right there in front of me!

Then I noticed little Gonzalo peeking out from behind the cart on the street. My stride was indignant, my voice shaky and my red face showed my disgust. I said to him, "Did YOU do that?"

He cowered down behind the wheel and murmured softly, "Yeah, Mama told me to."

His mother had been trying to get us out of the neighborhood. Her unbridled religious fanaticism was unequaled.

Because of this, Bill and our colleagues, the Zambranos, went to the airport without me. I got a pail of warm, sudsy water, lots of rags and newspaper, another pail of clear water and the mop. Then I beckoned to Gonzalo. He was scared but came to stand beside me. A four-year-old isn't very efficient with rags and mops, but he did his best, sniffling and grunting the whole time. Our guests detected no stain. No longer was there a bad odor. Gonzalo, himself, stood in the street door to greet them in clothes that resembled weird rags, with a dirty smiling face and very clean hands. I was amused by their exclamation,

"Oh, how adorable" and "Isn't he sweet?" Inside, I was chuckling.

## 49 LET'S TEST MY FLEXIBILITY, AGAIN! (1971)

Christmas is my favorite time of year. In Cuenca, it was a significant occasion to demonstrate love, especially to the children. Our neighbor children were fascinated with our Christmas tree. Some came every day, basking in the loveliness of the decorations and sniffing delightful pine fragrance. The afternoon of the twenty-fourth, I hustled and bustled to get everything ready. Guests were expected as usual. This time, we were having both baked chicken and roasted guinea pig. It was our son's last Christmas before going to the States for college.

I needed a little nap. I lay on the bed, looking out the big window to the purple, blue mountains, thinking about the music for the worship serice we would soon sing in the little store front church. Then we would have the dinner celebration that would last until after midnight, as usual. There was an urgent knock on the door. Something was wrong, it seemed by the sound of that knock. I hurried to open the door, only to find a "hoard" of children before me, each one with an expectant smile. Maria held a small bunch of flowers for me. No one asked permission to enter. They just moved en masse intot he hallway and on into the living room where the tree graced the front corner. They all flopped down on the floor, facing the magnificent tree. "Oh mira, es maravilloso!" (Oh, look at it, it's marvelous.)

I looked down to where they had marched in. Muddy prints splotched my shining wood floor. They just sat there, looking and looking and looking. One of the bolder boys approached the cookie candyhouse I had made and said, "Remember that you said that we could taste it?" I had thought I would share it on the twenty-seventh, which was my birthday because I wanted it as part of the Christmas Eve decorations for now. Pepe, the bold one, leaned forward to remove the cellophane. Their pleading expressions gave me no choice. They crowded closer. No one was there with a camera to even record my culinary accomplishment before this darling little hoard began to devour it.

Only a bit of the roof was left for Robertito, the pastor's toddler son. The kids dotted the floor with crumbs, their grubby hands sticky with frosting, after which they characteristically trampled on the crumbs on the way to the door, smiling their "thank you". Most of them hugged me. They all trouped out the door, chattering about the experience, hollering out, "See you later in church!"

"Whew!" I let out a sigh. I didn't know whether to be glad I'd shown love to the kids or disturbed that I had to clean up the mess before getting ready for church. I decided to do the latter chore using that as a time to pray for the boys and girls. That made me smile, remembering the whole scene, their delight and their satisfaction. After all, what WAS my job, grabbing a broom and mop or learning to be FLEXIBLE yet again? In God's order of things, it turned out to be both!

# 50 WHO IS MY NEIGHBOR? (1972)

On a Thursday morning in October, I asked myself that question as I drew back the curtain of our guest room in Cuenca to look down on the cobblestone street below. The scene was quite unlike any street back in Ohio.

Little Gonzalo sat picking his nose, fascinated by an Indian woman who milked her goat nearby. The carpenter and his helper clumsily arranged chairs on the sidewalk to begin their sanding. Black-haired boys and girls skipped by, jauntily swinging their twill school bags. Matilde emptied her dishpan into the street, seemingly oblivious to her toddler's whining as he shivered in the brisk morning air. Don Vicente picked up a piece of rubber tire and whacked angrily at his two sons. Evidently, they hadn't scrubbed his bus to his satisfaction. Maria squatted before her mountain of bread, apparently too sleepy to work at selling it. Ana's mother, the aristocrat down the street, stepped out of her Datsun, pulling on blue kid gloves.

I thought of the childhood ditty: "Rich man, poor man, beggar man, thief." They all seemed to be there in our neighborhood.

"Love your neighbor as yourself," Jesus said. So our hearts cried, "Lord, help us demonstrate your love to these neighbors." God responded, as He always does. The neighbors—the lonely, the sick in mind, the poor, the social outcasts, the victims of greed—most of them living without faith in Christ, were part of our lives.

Lucila was the neighbor down the street. I was drawn to her bleak, forlorn expression. She still loved her ex-husband, even though they'd been divorced over for two years. Her mother saw her as a reproach to the family, her sister shunned her, and former friends called her "loose and easy". Lucila tried to drown her loneliness and heartache in liquor. Over coffee while shopping together one week, I talked about Christ's love for her. Then later, on a picnic in the country, Bill talked about that same love with her. Once she came to a Bible study in our home, but was embarrassed by the women's curious questions. A couple of nights later, a young man banged on our door around 10:30 p.m., "Come right away. Lucila is screaming for you," he urged.

I threw a coat over my robe and rushed down the street. Lucila's wide-eyed three-year-old couldn't understand her mother's writhing and crying. Though Lucila had called for me, she was too drunk to realize I was there. I prayed for guidance while cradling her in my arms. Soon she began to talk to God, "Hey, You up there, why don't You listen to me? I'm not real, real bad, just alone. Why can't You give me back my husband? Why must I hate life like this? God, You've got to do something." Over and over she repeated the last demand. The next morning, Lucia was at my door, scrubbed and grateful. Yet, when I talked again of the Way of Salvation, her hate and bitterness held her in their vise. I wondered, "Will she ever come to Christ?"

Thursday was market day in Cuenca. Indians from the nearby province of Canar squatted on the curbing, resting between errands. Bill and I were impressed to pray, "Lord, give us favor with them." The Spanish vocabulary of the Indians is usually limited to market terms. Nevertheless, Bill, with his friendly smile, gave out simply written tracts. The Indians were reluctant to talk with him.

One Thursday at lunchtime, we heard a hesitant knock at the door. Two Indians wanted to talk with Bill. They filled Bill's ears with their story of being victimized by wealthy hacienda owners who paid only thirty-five cents a day for hard field labor. The motive of their visit was this, "Please, Señor Bill, give us 10,000 sucres ($400.00) so we can buy our own land." Bill's answer was biblical, " I don't have many sucres, but I have a real treasure to share with you—the Lord Jesus Christ, our Savior."

The Indians listened for a while and left. They kept coming each week. I don't know if they kept returning for the coffee and donuts or the cheese sandwiches we offered them, or if they were really hungry for the Word of God. It didn't matter what they came for, they got it all.

Another neighbor was Teresa. I didn't understand her very well, that is, I didn't understand her lifestyle. How could she live with that horrible man? They were not married. She was not bound to him. How could she leave her baby so dirty even though his chubbiness said she fed him well? How could she just sit in the sun and do nothing despite the fact that she had never gone to school for formal learning? My friendliness and an occasional pat on her shoulder seemed to help me communicate God's love to her. She began to tell me her heartaches and disappointments. Poor Teresa! Her overwhelming desire was to have another child—after five miscarriages and two stillborn babies! Her attention span to the Gospel story was very short.

Near the end of the year, I looked out on our street and realized how God had worked despite the discouraging days. After more than ten months of involvement with Lucila, we were happy by her conversion to Christ and subsequent baptism. As far as we know those Indians did not make a public profession of faith in the Lord, but there is now an evangelical preaching hall in their community. Maybe the seed we planted will come to harvest through someone else. Teresa finally agreed to attend the preaching services in the church. By the end of the year, she was known as a *simpatizante* (sympathizer) to the Gospel.

# 51 A LESSON IN PERSEVERANCE (1972)

We had been totally immersed in the direct evangelism necessary for church planting for more than a year in the small city of Cuenca. Almost every afternoon, Bill and the team of three Ecuadorians divided into two pairs and went door to door, praying for opportunities to witness their faith in the Lord, maybe sell a Bible, make an appointment for a return visit, or pray for a disturbed person. One particular week looked as though all was going to be a complete disappointment. They had knocked on doors, initiated conversations in the marketplace, stopped people on the road. Not one person responded positively. The fellows were discouraged.

"Lord, give us a family, or even just one person who will let us talk about Your message," Roberto prayed on Friday morning. Nothing happened that morning. After lunch they went out again to visit on the outskirts of town. They arrived at the very last cottage at the end of the very last street. Bill and Roberto looked at each other and almost gave up. However, since they had been learning more and more about perseverance in their labors, they knocked on the door.

"Buenas tardes," the smiling man in the doorway said to them. "What can I do for you?"

Roberto smiled in return as he answered, "We are interested in talking to people about preparing for heaven. Would you give us a few minutes to talk to you?"

"Come on in and sit down."

There was no obstacle. They got right to the serious business of explaining the Gospel. Mr. Pinos listened closely and then said, "Gentlemen, I read the Bible almost every day. There are some things that perplex me, but I keep on reading. By the way, I teach some high school classes here in the town."

An hour later he prayed in remorse for his sin and received Jesus Christ as his Savior. The following week, his wife and oldest teenage son accepted the Lord. Within two months, the other four children were also converted.

What if Roberto and Bill had given up and gone home that Friday afternoon when they were discouraged? Mr. Pinos became an elder in the newly formed church. His son, Johnny, was called to preach, went to Bible Institute and became pastor of the very church where he was baptized.

## 52 SIGHT COMES TO ANTONIO (1972)

While getting the church started in Cuenca in 1972, three college students, Pam, Charles, and Bev (who was my youngest sister) were helping in the summer activities and joined me for a day of sightseeing in Quito, the capital. We climbed into the wooden bus and went to the Equator Monument outside the city. The trip was uneventful on the way there. Time walking around the shops and snack stands was also without incident. I drew the young people into a circle in the shadow of the pillars to pray together that God would give us an opportunity to talk to someone about our faith in the Lord Jesus Christ.

I took a seat in the front row of the bus to return to the city. One space was vacant beside me. When I heard the tap, tap of a blind person's cane I looked up inviting the young blind man to sit beside me. He sighed and with visible fatigue settled into his seat, the white cane resting between his knees. I initiated the conversation as we started the journey. He was very young and I was older. There was no breach of etiquette in my beginning the dialogue. We talked about his need for a job, his ailing mother, his desire for Braille reading material. I told him about my husband, our son, my family far away, and my faith in Christ. That struck a chord in his heart and he responded to my witness immediately. While the bus lumbered down the cobblestone road to the city, Antonio and I talked about the Lord and His love.

"How can I expect God to give me salvation? I'm just a poor, blind man. I've had very little schooling, I've nothing to make me worthy of His attention."

"Listen to me, Antonio. You want peace in your heart and the assurance of heaven, do you not?"

"Si, si, sure I do. But I'm just a nobody," he answered.

"Precisely, Jesus came to save sinners, to give His love to the 'nobodies'."

Pam spoke up from the seat behind us, "I think we have to get off soon, Lois."

My companions had been listening to our conversation and praying for me. Although Antonio did not understand Pam's English, he sensed that I was moving to gather up my packages. He said, "I'll get off here with you and you can tell me more about this love of Jesus for the 'nobodies'."

We five stood on the sidewalk while I finished relating the story of Christ's sacrifice on Calvary. Antonio surprised us when he said, "Well, I can tell God about my sins and repent and tell Jesus I want Him to be my Savior right now, right here, can't I?"

He dropped to his knees there on the cement. We joined him, rather self-conscious I have to admit, as we heard him pour out his heart to God. I asked God's blessing on his life. Antonio stood to his feet with a big smile and an even bigger hug. Bystanders were curious, but that didn't disturb Antonio since he couldn't see them!

After a visit to HCJB, the Gospel radio station, where Antonio met a person who would help him find the Bible in Braille, we four continued our sight seeing. Our "seeing" that day was enhanced by the experience of Antonio coming to receive his spiritual vision.

# 53 THE TORMENTOR WAS FORGIVEN (1972)

"Come on, guys, you can throw better than that. We'll never scare these heretics away with that little smattering of pebbles." Oswaldo scolded his companions in his project of chasing us away. He picked up a large stone, drew back with a scornful laugh and threw with all his might, right at the window of the little split-bamboo church.

"Three cheers for our boss man," Pepe hollered, and followed his leader's example.

The next morning, Oswaldo spied Marta and me who usually stopped to talk to his mother. "They have no right to be in this neighborhood," he told Pepe. His hands filled with rotten vegetables from the trash bin. He took aim and "split-splat", the tomatoes hit the target. Oswaldo laughed again as Marta and I dabbed at our stained dresses.

His strutting steps, his smoldering black eyes, his jutting chin and the smirking expression gave clear evidence that he hated those Gospel people invading his territory of the red light district in Guayaquil. His mother shouted, "Go to it, boy, get them away from here."

"Yeah, mama, I'm doing my best. But they don't pay much attention to our protests."

"Don't you worry, my boy, we'll have that little church closed in a couple of weeks. Just keep up your good work."

Weeks later, even though Oswaldo and his buddies had practically ruined the roof of the little church and despite the times he had dirtied the skirts of the "Gospel women" with garbage, the church was still open for business. To their chagrin we kept on visiting in the district.

One day, Oswaldo's mother was beaten by one of the men in a drunken fit. Oswaldo was furious. Just then, we walked up with the pastor of the little church, who saw the bleeding, bruised woman and hurried to her side. "Now, Estela, everything's going to be O.K.," the pastor said, "God loves you. He's caring for you. We're going to take you to the clinic. The nurses there will treat you kindly. Don't worry. We've been praying for you and your son every day. God will take care of you."

A few weeks following that, Estela said to her son, "Oswaldo, those people can't be bad because they've treated me so well. They really seem to love us. They keep telling me that God loves us."

"Mama, you aren't talking right. We can't listen to their words."

"Well, son, I'm already listening."

"You say that God loves us, that those people love us?"

"I'm reading about God's love in that little booklet. They gave you one, too. Remember? It is called the Gospel of St. John."

Soon after Estela was healed, she cried to God with the pastor by her side, "Oh, Lord, I'm a terrible, terrible sinner. I confess to you my evil ways. I leave this old life. Forgive me. Forgive me. Give me a new life."

Estele was forgiven, loved and forgiven. Oswaldo laughed, "I know my mother! She won't last!"

Five years later, I was sitting in the hotel lobby in Cuenca helping to register young men and women for the young people's retreat. A young man fell to his knees before me and blurted out, "Oh, forgive me, please forgive me."

"Who are you?" I asked.

"I'm Oswaldo. Remember your tormentor of the red light district? Please forgive me for the very bad way I treated you. You'll forgive me, won't you? God has changed my life."

"Of course, Oswaldo, I forgive you," I said, my eyes glistening with tears. "We can't let anything stop the flow of Christian love, can we? You're forgiven and you're loved."

When we returned to Ecuador in 1998, it was really exciting to hear that Oswaldo was a faithful servant of the Lord, a preacher in fact, in Guayaquil.

# 54 GOD HELD BACK THE DARK CLOUDS (1972)

God uses negative happenings to encourage church growth! What happened in Cuenca is a good example of that. It was a perfect night for being cozy inside the house. Enoe, our Ecuadorian friend, and I were cutting out figures for the next children's Bible club to the rhythm of the "pit-pat, pit-pat" of the heavy raindrops on the metal roof. Bill and the evangelism team went out to the nearby country colony to Pepe's house. Several people were now regularly attending the Friday night Bible study there.

When Bill left the house I expressed my wariness because of the threats they had received. Certain people didn't want Bill or the Gospel team in their territory. Last week, a smattering of stones on Pepe's roof were supposed to serve as a warning. Our son, Billy, came from afternoon errands. We three discussed the threats. Then I noticed the hour. It was getting late! I was concerned. Where were the men? Had something happened? Billy went out to the street to investigate. At that moment, the younger men of the team arrived at our house, panting, pale and shaken.

"At first we had a good time at Pepe's house," Roberto said. "About ten people from the colony joined us. As Guillermo (Bill) was finishing the study, the stones began to hit the roof and we could just feel the hatred behind them. Someone looked out the window. The rain had stopped. We all looked out then and saw a great crowd of fellows, most of them drunk. They shouted obscenities. The boys and I wanted to escape. Since the study was over, we grabbed our jackets and rushed out the back door running down the muddy lane to the highway. We didn't want any part of a stoning."

"Well, where are Bill and Luis, the older believer from up north?" I asked.

Roberto hung his head in shame, "I guess we should have stayed to help them. But we were scared!"

We made a circle of prayer asking God to protect Bill and Luis. Then the door was pushed open. Bill fell to the floor before us, his raincoat all dark and stained.

"Oh, there's so much blood!" I exclaimed.

Thankfully, I discovered that most of the stains were only mud. It had been raining for fifteen days. The roads and paths were squishy and thick with reddish, brown mud. Before we took Bill to the clinic for treatment of his bruises, we listened to his story which was interspersed with sighs and long pauses.

"After the boys left us, the attackers became earnest in their intent to destroy Pepe's house. They fully intended to harm us as well. Luis ran out the back door. I don't know where he is. I calmed Pepe's wife and helped move the furniture to the center of the room to cover it because there were by that time, many broken roof tiles and water was leaking in. The rain had stopped, thank the Lord. I tried to leave by the back door but it was blocked by drunken men. Pepe sat huddled with his whimpering wife and crying children. Choked with emotion he said, "If you go now, brother, they'll probably leave us alone." There were attackers at the front door, too. I put my violin case up to protect the back of my neck and ran. Halfway down the lane, I stumbled and fell in that terrible mud. Then the stones came hard and heavy at me. I'm a little hurt." Thank the Lord, the violin case had protected his head.

While Bill struggled to his feet out there on the muddy path, a small truck came in from the highway. The burly driver scolded the attackers. He helped Bill get into his cab and brought him back to town to our house. A few minutes later, Luis, the older team member, arrived. He had hidden in the cornfield. He had time to count the attackers. The moon was rather bright above the dark clouds, bright enough to make out the figures of more than fifty inebriated young men, shouting horrible threats against the "heretics".

Later, while Bill lay in bed, having been treated for the many bruises on his back, the evangelism team and I stood by the big window. We were all worried about the black clouds that were rolling in from the mountain range. We never "interfere" to pray for the climate to change except to pray for protection from the elements. This time all of us were concerned enough to make an exception to that general rule. Almost every tile of Pepe's roof was broken by the stones that had been hurled against it. His little home would be ruined if the heavy rains started again to pelt down on that porous, fractured roof. I said, "Our only answer for this moment is to pray."

"Dear Lord, hold back the black clouds. Be merciful and keep the rain away until the men from the church can repair Pepe's roof."

The next day, the men from the congregation worked hard on the repair job. About twenty minutes after the last tile was put in place the rains came. All was safe! Some of the people of Cuenca, including that kind truck driver and the taxi driver who had brought the team back to our house, indignantly encouraged Bill to make a legal charge against the attackers. No such action had entered his mind. Everywhere we went, people were talking about the incident.

As we looked back, we determined that the stoning marked the beginning of the growth of the new church and an uplifting atmosphere of spiritual fervor on the congregation. It was sort of strange. As Bill lay on the bed, feeling sore and tired, his heart felt very calm and was filled with a joy that he couldn't describe. We came to the conclusion that his joy and serenity were a normal reaction for the persecuted believer. Amazingly, God gives joy through suffering, serenity through turmoil. What an amazing God we serve!

# 55 PERSECUTION (1972)

Toward the end of the year it seemed that the opposition had lessened there in Cuenca. The angry mother of the little boy across the street stopped sending him to urinate at our door. For seven weeks, I hadn't heard any shouts of "devil" as I walked down the street to the market. The candle-bearing, fervent devotees no longer paused in their procession down our street to pray the Rosary before our building. Not even one little pebble was aimed at Bill and the Crusaders in their street meetings. I remarked to Roberto, our pastor, "This seems too good to be true."

Nelson Pinos and I wrote a Bible drama for our young people to present—both in our little church and in a rented hall on the other side of town. Someone who had special favor with the TV administrator achieved an outstanding opportunity for us. He arranged for us to give the complete drama on the Cuenca television channel in the early evening. Just hours before we had to appear, I laid out the costumes and reviewed everything with the participants. Martita was not present! We needed her! She was Mary, the "star" of the show. While Nelson continued the rehearsal, I quickly walked over to Martita's home. My urgent knock brought an immediate response. It wasn't Martita who answered the door however. It was her mother, her face red with blistering anger, spouting out at me, "You heretic. I will not let my Martita associate with you any longer!"

She reached behind her for an ironwood rod, lifted it into the air and shouted, "Get away from here, go away, go away! Or I'll beat you!"

With great disappointment, I turned to walk away. My walking became running when she proceeded to come after me with that rod! Fortunately for me, she only succeeded twice to whack my shoulder.

That left us with a big problem. We had no Mary! Our delightfully creative God had another plan. One of the younger women who had been assigned a role helping with the props and other little jobs was not only interested but keen enough to have already memorized both Mary's and another woman's smaller part! She very ably stepped in on the spur of the moment. All I had to do was to hem up the skirt of her tunic. Satan was thwarted! The "persecution" gave no ill result. In fact, we were even invited to give the drama in the local high school.

## 56 BLESSED ARE THEY WHO ARE FLEXIBLE FOR THEY SHALL NOT BE ETERNALLY BENT OUT OF SHAPE! (1973)

"I don't have room in my heart for Spaniards. Even though I've been putting articles and statistics about Spain in a file, I have no inclination to go to Spain." My statement to Bill was very clear upon reading the letter we received from the OMS Board requesting that we help to make up the pioneer team to open ministry in Spain.

"Well, to be true to OMS, we have to pray seriously about it and then give them an answer," Bill wisely responded. The following week, he was scheduled to go to the coast where an Every Creature Crusade was being held. We decided that each would pray about the possible future assignment while we were separated. My sister, Nancy Kime, and her surgeon husband along with their charming children had only been in Saraguro a couple of months. My heart was filled with joy to have her near. I couldn't picture myself traipsing off to another country at this time. Therefore, my prayers were quite passive at first. I turned to the Bible. Reading from the book of Isaiah jolted me into a more active attitude of obedience. I was not very happy with the direction my heart seemed to be taking me. It was very disconcerting how often my thoughts traveled to Spain.

Bill returned to Cuenca late Saturday night. Our attention to other people was so necessary, that we had no time to talk about our prayerful decisions until after the morning service. Bill and I started to walk home just a few blocks away. He took my hand and asked, "Have you come to a decision about Spain?"

I gulped replying tearfully, "I'm afraid so, but I don't particularly like it."

Bill said, "When I was praying and reading the Bible, the Lord clearly showed me through Isaiah 6:8, that we should answer 'yes.' The church here is showing maturity and Roberto is capable of leading the congregation. "How about you, dear?"

"Well, maybe you'll be surprised, but I was reading Isaiah too, and the Holy Spirit impressed me to answer that question, 'Who will go?' so I think we should go to Spain." God had given us another experience of transition to learn about flexibility.

The Cuenca believers responded to the announcement about leaving with dismay. One leader asked, "How will we get along without you?"

Another declared, "I don't think we're ready for you to leave."

Bill and I prepared an exhortation for them for we wanted them to understand that even though they were feeling inadequate to be "on their own," God in His sovereignty and mercy had been grooming them for this next step. II Corinthians 3:1-6 emphasizes that our competency comes from God. We read this to them, endeavoring to control the emotion tearing at our hearts. "Dear brothers and sisters," we said, "there is a kind of blessing in feeling inadequate for a task from the Lord. We're going to Spain, not feeling very adequate to encounter a new culture. These feelings of inadequacy can drive us to depend all the more on the Lord." I noticed the people sat up straighter and gave good attention to this new thought. "When we feel inadequate but have the responsibility to serve the Lord, we are relieved of the burden of doing the will of God in our own strength. This feeling of inadequacy forces us to seek guidance, teaching, and power from the Holy Spirit. That is encouraging, is it not?"

We continued, "When we feel inadequate and know we ARE inadequate in our own strength, God provides the blessing of demonstrating the great things He can do with so little. INADEQUACY DOES NOT MEAN UNUSABLE. It is very bad to say, 'I know I can handle this.' Whatever would pull you dear ones away from depending on God and His promises is disastrous. Being inadequate means that you are freed for God to use you to the maximum of your potential."

Roberto, the pastor, stood and although his voice was choked with tears, he said with a smile, "We are going to trust even though we acknowledge our inadequacy. We claim God's adequacy by faith."

"Amen," responded the congregation. Little did we know at that time that it was not only our flexibility that was to be tested.

# SPAIN

Dr. Benjamin Pearson wrote: "The miracles of Spain have been and are no accident. They are the fulfillment of long stratagems of the Spirit; of providences so abundant and so intricate that only God could have woven them."

## 57 OUR INITIATION TO MADRID (1973)

Bill and I had enlisted several hundred people to fast and pray regarding our entry into Spain on August 25, 1973. Dad Miller had prayed this at our farewell in Cleveland:

> "Oh, Lord, may Bill and Lois be sensitive to the Holy Spirit's suggestions in even the complex, perplexing circumstances of the future. We thank thee that thy hand is upon their lives in a very specific way."

We stopped in England en route to Madrid along with Jeannine Brabon. The morning of our flight to Spain, in the home of the Kents, Mabel Callender's sister, we enjoyed the lovely rose garden within sight of Windsor Castle. I was disappointed though, that Harvey, the big white rabbit that usually insisted upon coming into the house to greet everyone in the morning, couldn't be found. The flight was uneventful. As we approached Spain and looked down on its dry plateaus and scenic mountains, the impressive cities broke into our sight. We three held hands and prayed, mostly exclaiming "hallelujahs."

As we left the plane, I looked up to the observation roof. I was sure I saw tall Burt Biddulph and waved excitedly to him, throwing a kiss to the woman beside him. Imagine my consternation when I found out that it wasn't Burt! No one of the mission team was there to meet us. It was a Saturday afternoon and none of the phone numbers on our list gave a response. We refused to be downhearted. Jeannine went out for a walk around the building while I guarded the luggage. Bill continued to make phone calls while he happily started a conversation with a Spaniard about the Gospel. How typical of him! The Lord trusted us with almost eight hours of waiting! Jeannine perched on the low table beside our divan and read aloud to us from her paraphrased Bible. Psalm 27 encouraged us.

When we finally loaded our luggage into a small taxi, I didn't know whether to cry or giggle. We had Ruben and Lidia Gil's home address but upon arriving there, the house was dark. Bill went to the door to check it out. Jeannine went to the neighbor's gate where finally someone responded. She remarked, "It is just like any other large city. Everyone minds their own business. So, now what?"

Going from hotel to hotel, and not finding a room because it was in the height of tourist season increased our perplexity. I found encouragement when the Spirit brought to mind Dad Miller's farewell prayer. Finally, we found a little, actually a really TINY room for the three of us together. That is what you call "instant bonding"! We were glad we had each other. We were neophytes to the culture. At eleven o'clock at night, throngs of people milled about the cafes and sidewalks. The air smelled like olive oil, garlic, and an unusual perfume. It accentuated our hunger and we ate our supper at midnight.

The jet lag contributed to our desire for sleep so we weren't surprised when Jeannine whispered out at 10:15 the following Sunday morning, "Maybe it's time to get up." There was no church service that day for us but our consciences didn't even prick us a little bit. We fasted breakfast and got out on the street about three o'clock for our second Spanish meal. Either my palate was already becoming accustomed to the olive oil, or the cook was not so generous as the previous night's chef. During the afternoon, Bill made more than twenty attempts on the telephone. Not even the U.S. Embassy officer had any information regarding the whereabouts of our team members.

Monday morning, with bags packed and everything in order, our hearts pounded with excitement over the prospect of finding our OMS missionaries. This time, it was Jeannine who went to the phone to call the number we had for the OMS office. Mary Gillam answered. We were out of that hotel with the speed of lightning! The Biddulphs and Mary felt badly about our dilemma, much more than we. Everyone had gone to a conference in England, thinking they'd see us there. The mail system was faulty so they had received no word from us about flight plans.

Burt Biddulph, our field director, in his gentle, concerned attitude blessed us from the very beginning. There was no moment of feeling ill-at-ease. It was pleasing and edifying to meet as a team for prayer and praise, for meals around the table, for excursions directed by Ruben Gil so that we'd get better acquainted with our new country. My heart began to stretch. There was no problem in making more room for God's servants and the Spaniards who needed Jesus so badly.

We soon realized that behind the lace mantillas, the colorful singing, the strumming of guitars, and the impressive display of art and culture of modern Spain were sorrowing, aspiring people, often suppressed by social and religious systems and battered by class struggles. Only one out of every one thousand Spaniards at that time was a Protestant—one-tenth of one percent! The Spanish Protestant believers constituted what was probably the smallest evangelical minority in any country in the western world we were told. Our initiation into the Spanish culture had to include the study of the history of the church. During the bloody years of the sixteenth century, Spain's Roman Catholic Inquisitors ruthlessly stamped out "the Protestant heresy" and the "Christ killing Jews". No one knows how many thousands lost their lives. There is no record of any surviving Protestant group.

In 1868 however, a liberalizing tendency appeared and a few of the men who had been exiled because of their views returned. A few small groups for Bible preaching began to be formed in the major cities. The modern history of Protestantism in Spain actually dates from the period immediately after the Spanish Civil War, 1936 to 1939. The effect on Spain and on evangelicals in particular was devastating. Only a handful of families and a few pastors survived, and they were scattered all over the peninsula. Little by little, however, congregations gathered, pastors were trained, missionaries from England, Germany and the U.S. arrrived and congregations were established. At first, the believers were only allowed to meet in homes with a limit of twenty people in attendance. Restrictions were relaxed but Protestants were not allowed to build structures that looked like churches or even put up a sign identifying themselves as a congregation and they were not allowed to erect a cross on the exterior of a building. From a mere handful in 1939, the evangelical population grew to a noteworthy 30,000 by 1973.

In 1967, a law regarding religious liberty was passed in the Spanish parliament. The "non-Catholic confessional associations" had to submit membership lists, financial statements, a statement of belief, and other data to the Ministry of Justice who would then give official recognition to a non-Catholic congregation or denomination.

You can imagine the hesitancy and suspicion of our new Spanish neighbors. We surely could not stand on their doorstep and declare, "Here we are, you lucky people." We needed to make contacts, establish friendships, get close to the people. We prayed for that to happen.

# 58 OUR FIRST FRIENDLY NEIGHBOR (1973)

Everywhere I looked in the Chamartin neighborhood of Madrid where we found our first apartment, I noticed well dressed, attractive women. One petite woman and I often crossed paths in the lobby of the apartment building and smiled at each other. That in itself was special because the people here did not return a smile very easily. The janitor told us, "You'll have to live here two years before people begin to loosen up."

One afternoon, Bill came in after studying neighborhood statistics in the government office and said, "I talked with Irene, our neighbor on the next floor down. She's the small one who always dresses so fashionable—the one you remarked about. She has to have some injections and somehow I let her know that I can give them. So I'm going down pretty soon to do it for her." As I sat at the typewriter, I didn't feel very comfortable about Bill's going down there alone. "O.K., I'll go with you."

Irene opened the door to us, dressed in a loose and flowing chiffon negligee. She quickly recovered her surprise at seeing me beside my husband and made me feel comfortable. That was the beginning of a rather superficial friendship in which I always took the initiative for us to have coffee together. I prayed for the opportune moment to introduce the claims of Christ. When it did arrive, Irene stood to her feet, slamming her coffee spoon down on the table. "Listen to me, Lois, you know how I earn my money, I'm not ready to close the door to my clients nor am I ready to become an old fuddy-duddy Christian. You can leave and not ever return."

I couldn't even hug her goodbye. Yes, of course, I knew that she was a prostitute and a very popular one. I also knew that she needed Jesus more than any man. I had told her that He wanted to be her Savior, Healer, and Friend. After that day, she avoided me. She would cross the street when I was headed her way. Since she was aware of the Truth of the Gospel, I pray that one day, she will bow in repentance before the Savior who loves her.

# 59 THE CHAPLAIN CHANGED HIS MIND (1973)

A few months after arriving in Madrid, one of our new friends arranged for us to go to the U.S. Air Base outside of town to present a program of music and testimony. When the chaplain received us at the door, he was not very cordial. We went well prepared in our souls and in our music. The young military personnel and their wives were very responsive. We noticed some tears, some expressions of joy and conviction too, as we sang and expressed our testimony. After seventy-five minutes of sharing, we closed the program. There was a hush and then a couple of sobs. The chaplain slowly came forward, gave Bill a big bear hug, gripped my hand, then turned to the sixty-five young people. He said in a choked voice, "When I saw Bill and Lois come in tonight I thought, 'Oh, God, are these a couple of heavies? I judged them on sight with their instruments and their big smiles." He blew his nose and continued, "Bill and Lois, please forgive me. I was too hasty. God has used you tonight and I've been blessed."

Then he went to one of the fellows and said, "Joe, I've been badgering and bothering you for several weeks. That has been mean. Please forgive me."

That was the beginning of confession, prayer, spontaneous singing, tears, and hugs. One couple spoke up and declared that they were through with disobedience and that after their military service, they were going to the mission field. This was followed by four men and one girl saying the very same thing! My heart was pounding. I didn't hold back the tears of joy. What victories! Then a young mother raised her hand and spoke up. "I've got to tell you all something. Right here in my seat I've told the Lord that I want to be a real Christian and live for Jesus from now on."

Finally, a young Jewish fellow stood and said, "I was convicted when Lois sang about her Savior. I confessed my sin and my hypocrisy and I want to declare Jesus as my Savior and Messiah."

Bill and I sang "Hallelujah" all the way back to our apartment.

## 60 IT WAS RIGHT TO WRITE (1974)

I was amused that the most popular brand of jeans in Spain was "LOIS." But one morning, I glanced up at the billboard near the bus stop and shuddered inwardly, aghast. It introduced the "NEW JESUS JEANS', showing the rear view of two shapely girls in short, very tight cut-off jeans. Across their jeans flashed the phrase, "Follow Me".

Now this was in Dictator Franco's time. How did the company "get away with that" in such a traditionally religious country? That afternoon I sat at our desk, head bowed in prayer, fussing. Then I scolded myself, "Don't just sit here. Do something!"

So, I wrote three letters of protest, each one with different wording, with a different signature, but no false signatures. In Spain, I was "Loida Pankuch" for a woman legally maintains her maiden name. I was also "Lois Jean Miller" and "esposa de Guillermo Miller Youngberg (wife of William Miller). I persuaded two other women to write the same protest. I asked three prayer partners to pray with me.

A few days later the offensive advertisement was gone! Paul told the Thessalonians, "Never tire of doing what is right". I was totally right to write.

# 61 MY CHEEKS ACHED FROM SMILING (1974)

The first responsibility for OMS in Spain was to provide office space for the Iberian Congress on Evangelism planned for June 4-8, 1974. Iberian meant that both Portugal and Spain (the peninsula of Iberia) were included with Spanish Protestants as the hosts.

That required cooperating wholeheartedly with Ruben Gil, our colleague, who served as Executive Secretary for the Congress. This meant that Bill and I joined Burt and Bernadine Biddulph, Jeannine Brabon, and Mary Gillam, doing all sorts of thing—writing and folding letters, stuffing envelopes, answering the telephone, feeding guests, and PRAYING!!! Bill and I also provided music for churches all over Spain as we accompanied Rubin on his promotional trips.

The Congress was the first Protestant activity of large proportions ever to be attempted in Spain. We expected at least one thousand people to meet in the Palacio de Congresos or Palace of Congresses. The peninsula's Gibraltar like resistance to the evangelical presence softened as 1,200 delegates and observers assembled for the unprecedented event. I accepted the responsibility of a greeter/receptionist which meant that my smile had to be kept polished all day long. That first night, upon preparing for bed, I put Vick's VapoRub on my cheeks. They actually HURT from smiling!

The leading Madrid newspaper gave the Congress front page coverage. A television team filmed the entire first meeting, a documentary on Protestant customs and worship. One of the crew remarked, "This makes me think I should be an evangelical, but I don't know about that public baptism." The immense auditorium was crowded to the last seat in the balcony. Men were sitting on the broad steps down the side aisles. A Portuguese and Spanish choir covered the large platform. The administrator of the Palace was one of the guests of honor. He stood at the podium and said, "I have come through a progressive experience during your Congress. I started with ignorance of the Protestants. Then I became curious and from curious I went to knowing you. From knowing you I went to profound respect and from profound respect I went to genuine affection. When I see the face of a Protestant, I see a smiling face. This is the first Congress ever held here in which we have received no criticism, no demands, no protests. And I thought you were *Protestants!*" He received a tremendous ovation.

The magazine, **European Pulse**, gave a full page report. The last paragraph was:

> After Rev. Luis Palau's powerful presentation of the gospel on closing night, Lois Miller sang her last solo, a Spanish version of *Just As I Am*. Fifty-six persons quietly slipped out the side doors to meet with counselors. Even this was an innovation for some of the participating churches, but well received. Afterwards, ministers were heard discussing plans to invite Rev. Palau for city-wide union evangelistic services. On two counts this is exciting news: that pastors are considering cooperation between denominational churches in united services and that pastors are committing themselves to public evangelism. So the miracle begun with the opening service of the First Iberian Congress on Evangelism continues.

It is no wonder that I kept smiling!

# 62 ASTRONAUT IRWIN SHARED HIS FAITH IN SPAIN (1975)

Colonel James B. Irwin, USA astronaut, told of the discovery voyage of Apollo 15 and gave testimony to his Christian faith to an audience of over two thousand people who packed the National Congress Palace in Madrid, May 28, 1975. Following the showing of his film, "High Flight", Irwin communicated the spiritual dimensions of his moon trip to an attentive crowd representing every social strata of Spain's capital city. An ex-general of the Spanish Air Force shook his hands and said, "It is a privilege to know you."

Ruben Gil, our OMS pastor, was president of the Madrid Ministerial Association at that time. He was responsible for organizing the meeting. As his assistant, I was privileged to work on it behind the scenes. The event, was not only highly significant, but it was also unprecedented in the history of the evangelicals in Spain which caused it to receive extensive press and television coverage, mostly favorable. Ten leading newspapers, along with national radio and TV, clearly identified Colonel Irwin as an evangelical minister. Others headlined him as "missionary from the moon". Most of the articles carried Irwin's testimony about a personal encounter with God through the Lord Jesus Christ.

How blessed we were to hear his comments about the Lord and to share a prayer time when he sat at our dinner table the next day. Mary Gillam called it a "serendipity". I heartily agreed.

# 63 NICHE #107 (1976)

One Sunday evening in October, 1976, about sixteen of us gathered around the piano after the service to sing hymns and choruses. I noticed Regina's bronze face shining as we sang about our friend, Jesus. Then she spoke up, "Let's sing number 286." It was new to many, but it was the expression of Regina's heart. Her tears spilled over as we sang the last verse:

>Jesús, sí llego a morir muy lejos de mi hogar,
>>Ni así podria tu sufrir mi vida compensar,
>
>Mejor amor de amigo jamás podré hallar,
>>Pos eso al Salvador oí decir.
>
>'Si solo un vaso de agua, te pido que has de dar,
>>De ti un vaso de agua, solo he de demandar.
>
>Mas si en tus aflicciones un alma has de ayudar,
>>De ti muy cerca yo prometo estar'".

O Jesus, if I die upon a foreign field some day,
'Twould be no more than love demands—
>No less could I repay;

'No greater love hath mortal man
>Than for a friend to die'—

These are the words He gently spoke to me:
'If just a cup of water I place within your hand,
Then just a cup of water is all that I demand:'
But if by death to living they can Thy glory see,
I'll take my cross and follow close to Thee. [1]

Joel, a new believer in the Tabernacle, represented all of us as he prayed and praised the Lord. (The Tabernacle had been established by the pioneer OMS team which included Burt Biddulph as the Field Director along with his wife Berna, Mary Gillam, Ruben and Lidia Gil, Jeannine Brabon, Bill and I). Everybody gave a Christian holy kiss, a custom in Spain, as we hugged prior to leaving for our respective homes. Reginas returned to the luxurious home where she served as housemaid since her arrival from Honduras.

The following Sunday we were all together again. Regina took a couple of us missionary women aside and said, "I need your help. For two nights I've been crying to the Lord, telling Him I need relief from the tension of my job. When I came here from Honduras, I had no idea that the people would be cruel to me. My employer shouted, 'Prostitute!' because I came in late last Sunday evening after our Gospel songtime. All week long I've been too scared to open my mouth. Everything I do or say is wrong. They haven't given me my full salary either. I don't know why they keep back twenty dollars more than my contract states. I have to work two full years to reimburse my airfare here. I don't know how long I'll have to work to get enough to return to Tegucigalpa. My parents don't really know about my heartache here. I have a diploma from an institute in Honduras. I worked as a laboratory technician there. Do you think you could get me a job here in Madrid, either as a helper in a lab or as a maid? Maybe I'll have to sneak out of that home. They treat me as though I were their slave!"

Her black, brown eyes glistened with tears. I put my arms around her. "I pray all the time, " she continued."That is the only way I get enough strength to get through every day. Help me, sisters, please help me!"

Later that night, Regina stepped down off the bus directly into the path of a speeding auto. Her life was ended, instantly. She carried no identification or was it taken from her? Only the little Gospel hymnal beside her mangled body had a name on the inside page, "Regina" just her first name and a stamp that read, Tabernáculo Evangélico (Evangelical Tabernacle). The police finally located the OMS office. Her card file of the Tabernacle revealed the address of her employer. Then the trouble began!

Regina was part of a devilish plan devised by greedy men who brought four hundred girls from Honduras to Spain. Their contracts were not legal. The girls paid more than double the necessary amount of their fares, they had very few privileges and they worked between seventy-six and ninety hours a week. Most of them got only Sunday night free and one hour an afternoon during the week. We heard the ambassador from Honduras promise to notify Regina's parents. Her mother was blind and her father confined to a wheelchair because of paralysis. Both were 'simpatizantes' or sympathizers to the Gospel, but had not made a public confession of faith to the Lord Jesus. The letters we wrote to her family tried to convey our compassion and prayer concerns for them.

Several of Regina's girlfriends pleaded with their employers and so were freed for several hours in order to view the corpse, but none of us were able to see it. Regina's body had been horribly broken. Burt Biddulph, Bill and Lidia Gil accompanied them to the morgue. The girls told them that no one had bothered to wash Regina; she was just crammed into a plastic bag! Later, several of the patronas (employers) shouted in anger at Lidia and Bill when they took the girls home, accusing them of interfering in the matter. We were in Spain to give the Gospel and to get people established in the Word of God, but we could not, as true believers, permit this injustice to continue.

The ambassador advised that Regina's body would be shipped home but to our horror when Ruben Gil went to inquire about the details of shipment he discovered that her body had been buried on the edge of the cemetery early that very morning. No one had been notified. Ruben was speechless that in such a strong Roman Catholic country as Spain, not even a priest had been summoned when they laid her twisted body to rest. Regina's passport, clothing, and what little possessions she owned had been buried with her in a cheap, crude box.

Regina was gone. Gone to a glorious place. Yet, how many girls remained in Madrid in the same circumstances? A memorial service was held two weeks later at the Tabernacle on Sunday. The ambassador and his wife, the consul and his secretary, forty Honduran girls and some of the Spanish believers attended to pay her their respects.

The following day the leading Madrid newspaper carried a two-column story with the headlines: "SLAVE TRADE?...400 GIRLS FROM HONDURAS, DOMESTIC SERVANTS...FALSE CONTRACTS...UNFULFILLED CLAUSES...4,000 PESETAS ($66.00 U.S.) PROFITED ON EACH ONE."

Here are excerpts from that reporter's story:

> It was twelve o'clock when we walked into the Alcobendas Cemetery. Old, stained lime sacks and abandoned shovels; discarded overalls from the workmen; an open ditch. Further on we noticed the serenity of the atmosphere—multi-colored plastic flowers, and dedication plaques; 'Your parents won't forget you.' May you rest in peace, my husband.' 'A final goodbye.'
>
> Over to the left, in a high-ceilinged room—a large bundle of green plastic. It contained a 23 year-old girl from Honduras, mother of two little children. Her eyes were open to the immensity of death. We felt chills. A strong odor of formaldehyde brought on nausea. The nude, mutilated body, crudely sewn up, with ugly bruises and a broken head, invited us to meditate deeply.
>
> An important personage appears in this lamentable story. The pastor-evangelist, Ruben Gil of the Evangelical Tabernacle of Madrid. He called together several of these 'victims' from Honduras for this interview. Incredible, that in this age of conquering oceans and outer space, man has not been able to conquer his avarice.
>
> The eighth article of this contract signed by these girls specified that in case of her death, the body would be embalmed and sent back to her country, expense to be covered by the employer. The contract of Evelicia, Regina's friend, is only signed by her (No employer's signature.) It is not valid. I was present in the Tabernacle when Pastor Gil informed the girls of this. They are filled with fright.
>
> And now the unfortunate victim has been buried, rapidly and without ceremony. Placed in an anonymous grave, Niche #107. All this leaves an enormous question that interrupts my sleep. Is this a kind of white slavery?
>
> What has happened to these girls seems to say to me that humanity is not going forward, but rather receding.

Most of the girls got better treatment after that. Investigation continued to unveil the injustices. The agent in Tegucigalpa that had arranged all their travel was put in prison. Several of the girls continued to attend the Tabernacle. Three of them asked Jesus into their hearts. Mercedes gave profession in public baptism. Regina did not die in vain. The transformation of the girls who accepted the Lord Jesus crowned the achievement of bringing this atrocity to light.

---

[1.] Third verse of the Gospel song, "Follow Me" by Ira F. Stanphill, Singspiration, Inc. 1953. Used by permission.

# 64 EVERY HURDLE CONQUERED (1977)

Niggling details teamed up with bigger disappointments tried to rob the Resurrection Concert in the Madrid Tabernacle of its impact. Those hurdles flagrantly disturbed my peace! I cried from frustration as I sat by the window several times, praying and wondering what to do. I like to organize and put things together, so planning and preparing for the Concert was as much fun as cooking a birthday banquet for my husband. That was not the hurdle.

April was chosen for the Concert. Back in December, I invited a very talented couple from another mission to sing four duets, including a lovely Gounod Aria and Gaither's *The King is Coming*. On New Year's Day, I began choosing the music for the choir that would even sing a transposed *Hallelujah Chorus* from G. F. Handel's *The Messiah* along with a simplified Bach chorale. The only converted Protestant Christian in the Madrid TV choir, a resonant baritone, would sing two solos. For accompaniment I had a flute, a violin, a beautiful organ and a piano. I would only sing two verses of a Sicilian melody with a violin accompaniment. My major task was to coordinate and direct.

The eighteen members of the volunteer choir rehearsed fourteen times. Half of them needed individual tutoring sessions with me. Once a volunteer singer joined the group he was committed. A huge hurdle! A couple of teenagers peevishly complained about the "grueling" sessions. "You demand too much," they said. Every week, somebody had to be encouraged to keep singing. Another hurdle! Two baritones constantly sang off key so that meant more individual attention. Andres, the pianist, had to miss two final rehearsals because of illness.

More hurdles—the large banner declaring, "ALELUYA, CRISTO VIVE" (HALLELUJAH, CHRIST LIVES) didn't look right. There were too many "l's", so it had to be done over! The printer lost the invitation. I thought I had been very creative, but the newer one turned out to be even more attractive. By then, it was too late to mail the invitation so we gave them out personally to people. That was even more impressive and effective. The duet cancelled their participation. The best soprano's baby decided to be colicky during the early evening hours so she sadly informed me two days before the concert that she would not be singing. One of the better altos hacked and coughed with what ended up to be severe bronchitis. She dropped out. The flutist cancelled. Then, the baritone's soloist's wife called, "Zazo can't sing. I'm sorry. He can't even sing next week with the TV choir. He has laryngitis."

I sat down by the balcony window. The sky was blue and the birds were singing, but I felt gray, very gray. I wiped away my tears asking the Lord, "Well, what do I do now, right before the concert?" I wasn't accomplishing anything feeling like a martyr so I obeyed my husband's advice and picked out some appropriate solos. That afternoon, I tried to make stencils for the program, but the office typewriter's capital letters were not clear. So late that night there I was using the typewriter at the Tabernacle!

The next day, we arrived at the Tabernacle, excited about our final practice. Three keys on the piano twanged. Bill hurried off to find the piano tuner. Then the organ pedal wheezed. Was Virgilio, the organist ever dismayed. Bill waited all the next day for the organ technician. On the day of the concert, he arrived at three o'clock!

At home, I was more nervous than I had ever been before in Spain. I read through every promise in my little promise box. I paced the floor and read fifteen psalms aloud. I tried to sing my solos feeling my body shake like a tired old victrola. Bill didn't call. His lunch was getting cold. I couldn't get any response from the phone at the Tabernacle. The devil attacked my emotions. Bill had been tired and I was concerned that he get some rest. I could just picture him, flat on the floor of the church, passed out, with a heart attack and no one to help him. Imaginations are sometimes good things and sometimes a force to be reckoned with!

When Bill came home, about thirty minutes before the time we had to leave for the concert, I didn't know whether to hug him or scold him.

I started to scold, but no response. That turned into tears. He hugged me hard. We prayed together. He took a ten minute rest and put on his elegant suit. I was already dressed in my long, blue gown. We left the house, on time, and smiling. But I was still very nervous. I thought of trying to get some Valium or something that middle-aged women take for nerves but Bill wasn't in favor of that.

Three choir members showed up for the concert with head colds. I did not feel free to excuse them. We committed the whole thing to the Lord together. The choir sang well. Their quality was good…their facial expressions very communicative. They followed me implicitly. Debi Grout, a short-term missionary, sang her Handel solo beautifully. The violin was sweet, the organ solo was majestic with its swelling chords. I could almost hear the yelling crowd shout, "Crucify Him, Crucify Him". I sang with my whole heart I Know that my Redeemer Liveth.

The church was filled to capacity. New people there included a Conservatory professor, a French princess, a university teacher, some students from South America, a medical doctor, and young people from the neighborhood. One woman willingly arranged an hour for conversation with me about our faith in the risen Lord. One of the young fellows of the choir who had grumbled about my demanding so much said, "I complained about so many rehearsals, but what a wonderful satisfaction I've felt today. I was part of a group that gave the real Easter message from our hearts."

## 65 THE GIRL IN THE VELVET OPERA CAPE (1977)

"She's stunning! Wow! She could model for Vogue magazine!" I exclaimed to Bill as we watched a young woman sway down the sidewalk to a waiting taxi, her velvet cape swinging from side to side. We went on down the street to make our follow-up visit to a woman who had attended the previous Sunday's service in the Tabernacle. The vision of that beautiful, fashionably-dressed girl remained in my memory. The next day Bill and I prayed for her. She had come from the building just around the corner from the church.

We saw the "glamour-girl" again, weaving from side to side up the walk to her entrance. Her drunken state was very evident and shocking since it was Saturday morning. The next Monday, Bill stood at the elevator door of the second floor of her building. He had just delivered some cassette tapes to one of her neighbors. The elevator stopped and out stepped the girl of the opera cape, her arms full of groceries. Bill, the ever attentive gentleman, offered to help her. She accepted his extended hand to hold a bag while she searched for her key. After the bags were deposited on her kitchen table, he took an invitation to the Tabernacle from his coat pocket and handed it to her. She said, "Gracias. My name is Dolores. I'm not very interested in religious stuff, but thank you. You are not Spanish, are you?"

"No, I'm from the States."

"Yes, I thought so. I often go to New York and Boston on my flights. I'm a stewardess on Iberia Air Lines. I've even thought of going to live there, but my father isn't in accord with that idea. I need his financial help so the best I can do is live here by myself so I'm not under his surveillance all the time."

"My name is Bill Miller. My wife and I saw you the other night leaving the building. She admired your velvet evening cape."

"Oh, yeah, that's the cape I usually wear to the opera."

"May we come and talk to you about what you read in that brochure I just gave you?"

"Oh, sure. I'll be home Thursday evening this week."

That was the beginning of our witnessing relationship with Dolores, probably the most glamorous woman we met during those years in Spain. She usually dominated the conversation, telling us about her disgust for her domineering father, her disappointment with the men in her life, her boredom with her job, and her custom of drowning her feelings in whiskey and gin. The first time Bill gently interrupted her, wanting to tell her how the Lord could help her handle her problems and give her peace, she threw the glass containing her gin to the floor. But then she quickly apologized. The second time she reacted to us was via the telephone when I offered to go and pray with her. She had sounded so sad, so melancholic, so desperate. Her filthy language made the hair on my arms bristle with the shock!

Nonetheless, Dolores invited us in with a big smile several more times. During the last frustrating conversation with her, we sat on her sofa while she stood at the bar. I talked about my assurance of salvation based on the Word of God. Bill talked about his relationship with the Lord. He explained again about God's love, each person's need to repent and get right with God through accepting the Lord Jesus as Savior. I added, "Dolores, God has brought us into your life for a very good reason. Tonight you can come here beside us and pray with us to get rid of your bitterness and your sinfulness by confessing to Jesus. Now, right now, you can have peace that you've never known."

"That does it! Don't you dare tell me I can't handle my problems! Don't you dare tell me I'm a sinner. This drinking. I could stop any day I want to. My feeling toward my father, well, when he comes MY way—My sin? I have no more sin than the other people in this city!"

As she hollered the words, "I have no more sin…" she grabbed the half-filled bottle of gin and threw it at us. It hit the mirror above us, shattered onto the sofa and onto our clothing. Dolores sneered, "Get out. Get out.

I never want to speak with you again." She marched to the door, threw it open and with a wide sweep of her hand, bade us her final farewell!

Peace? Dolores didn't have peace! Her pride, her stubbornness, her bitterness, all those feelings, all that attitude were potent impediments to her coming to Christ. Although we continued to try, we never gained admittance to her apartment again. She had shut us out of her life. How many others like Dolores are blocking out the peace-giving Savior?

We have asked that question of ourselves often.

# 66 A POETESS RESPONDS (1977)

Forty girls from the Humanities class of the nearby Catholic Academy, along with their teacher, requested an "audience" with Ruben Gil, the pastor of the Tabernacle. They wanted to ask questions about "our different religion".

Bill and I arranged a table, attractively prepared with illustrated literature, Bibles and Gospel tracts, next to the wide-open double doors of the Tabernacle. (I was a bit unsure about the nun's acceptance of this!)

As the pastor answered the students' questions, I stood by the book table which was about ten feet from the sidewalk. Women with their shopping baskets, young mothers pushing strollers and students with their bookbags all passed by, some glancing my way. I responded with a nod and a smile. No one stopped.

A well-dressed woman, short of stature and a few years older than I, looked my way. I smiled and she came toward me. I asked, "Would you like to see the lovely Bibles we have for sale?"

Her answer surprised me. "Yes, I've been thinking about buying a small, manageable one." She chose the most expensive one and said, "I'll begin reading today. Literature is very important to me."

God gave me boldness and I said, "I would be very happy to visit you in your apartment and read the Bible with you. It would be a pleasant experience." The Lord gave me favor with her. She informed me that she had her doctorate, having specialized in philology (the study of languages by the written texts known) and had just that year published a book of poetry for which she had received a medal of merit from the Royal Academy. To think that I had suggested to READ with her! Yet, the

Lord knew she needed His Word and a friend as well. I rarely missed going each week to Dr. Peña's house about ten in the morning leaving around two hours later during a period of about twenty weeks. She had many questions and was delighted to see how I used the Bible to cross reference the subject she was interested in. After a few weeks, I began to pray with her at the close of our reading session. She liked that.

Her husband, a retired colonel in the military, and a decorous gentleman, didn't appreciate the reason for my visit, but he was always courteous.

One day my new friend came very close to my side of the sofa stating firmly, "Now, Loida, don't ever invite me to your church. I would never think of entering a Protestant church. If you invite me, I'll feel sad. It would be discourteous to refuse your invitation which would offend you." In honor of her request I didn't invite her to the Tabernacle. I did make sure, however, that she understood Christ's invitation to faith in Him. Three weeks later she walked in before the Sunday morning service and sat next to me despite the fact I always sat up front in the second row!

Dr. Peña especially liked studying the personalities of the Bible. I had great fun listening to her new poetry about the women of the Bible. Missing her only daughter who was studying in the States at the Massachusetts Institute of Technology, she began calling me on the phone when she felt low in spirit. Sometimes the phone rang at midnight because she didn't understand a Scripture passage she was reading. After our conversation about the Bible, I always prayed for her.

My heart was happy the day she said she acknowledged Jesus Christ as Lord and personal Savior there in her home. She did declare, though, "I'll never be able to identify publicly with you. I wouldn't want to jeopardize my husband's position in the military."

She faithfully attended the Sunday preaching services and the women's Bible study group where she learned to pray with faith even though she never felt free to pray aloud in public. I thank God for the perseverance He gave me to keep returning to the house of the poetess.

## 67

# UNION FEMENINA EVANGELICA ESPANOLA
## The Evangelical Spanish Women's Union (1977)

"Lois, you just have to come to the meeting of U.F.E.E. with me. There's nothing like it. The Christian women here in Spain haven't had much opportunity to serve. Some are part of churches that give women the job of teaching the children and that's all. They don't even pray aloud in the prayer meeting. The men do everything. Then, my friend from Argentina and another woman prayed about encouraging the women, helping them to learn to use their gifts. The Lord led them to establish the Evangelical Spanish Women's Union in Barcelona. Now, we have chapters in several major cities. Please come. Your input will be a blessing." That is how Lidia Gil persuaded me to attend. She told me later that even then, she had in mind that I would be able to write the constitution they needed in order to make the organization a legal entity, which I did a year later.

The following week, as I sat drinking coffee with Violeta Campderros, one of the founders, I found myself promising to cooperate in some way with the Madrid chapter. That was the beginning of a journey of joy in service to the women of Spain.

Our major emphasis was a yearly retreat for worship, instruction seminars and companionship in prayer. The first year I attended, fifty-four women crowded the hotel meeting room. God blessed our promotional efforts. By the fourth year, we were ministering to two hundred women. That number had more than tripled by 1996 when Bill and I returned to visit our beloved field of Spain. God gave us wonderfully capable speakers, including Annze Graham Lot and Beatrix Zapata of Guatamala.

The Holy Spirit blessed my efforts as, on my knees, I put together the worship music for each conference. Loida Vangioni, president of

U.F.E.E., always gave the closing remarks and invitation at which time she expected a chorus or hymn from me. One woman observed, "It is absolutely uncanny—only proof of the Lord's sovereignty—how your music and Loida's remarks go together so appropriately." I loved working with Loida. My heart so bonded to hers that our being attuned to each other under the Holy Spirit's guidance seemed a normal thing.

Each major city, with its monthly meetings of encouragement, gave many women the opportunity to develop their skills in serving their Lord. I'll always cherish the memory of the "Bible Women Fashion Show." Twelve women represented outstanding Bible personalities dressed in well-researched, authentic costumes. Very few knew the prayers and labor behind those exotic tunics. We searched for an elegant gown, suitable for Queen Esther but to no avail. Lidia and I cried together in prayer about it one day. We probably could have found something in the bridal shop, but we didn't have eight hundred dollars! Anamaria Huck Vangioni, our OMS staff member in charge of the correspondence courses and the follow-up of the telephone ministry, was to be Esther. She was (and still is) beautiful. We knew that with her regal stance and loving face Esther was the very personality for her. We didn't have a suitable dress. One day, Lidia was in her backyard, hanging up sheets and towels. Her neighbor, seldom at home in the daytime, leaned over the fence to greet her and remarked, "You look sad. Is something wrong?"

"Yes, I'm worried. We can't find the right costume for the woman who will portray Queen Esther in our Bible Fashion Show. We're stymied and don't know what to do."

"Well, maybe I can help." She said. Lidia knew that she was the producer of special theme TV programs. Just the previous month, she had a great success with her presentation of ancient Syria.

"I've been trying to sell one of the costumes we used recently, but it is so ornate, so lovely, that only a very wealthy person would be interested. How would you like me to loan it to you?"

Lidia is a typical sanguine personality—expressive and emotional. She actually shouted, "Wonderful, wonderful! We'll take good care of it. We will. We will."

That problem was solved. It wasn't the only one, though! Where would we find the costume for the daughter of Pharaoh? The encyclopedia illustration could hardly be duplicated within our budget. "As for God, His way is perfect" (Psalm 18:30) proved its truth to us when a member of the Egyptian embassy facilitated a costume that took our breath away! Elida Barnett, with her high cheekbones and abundant hair, was a perfect Egyptian. She sat in the beauty salon for five hours while the hairdresser painstakingly braided and tied her hair.

We were then left to wonder about the last person in the procession, the Virgin Mary. Who would be willing to look pregnant? Since the program was to be given in the first week of December, it would be very fitting to close with a Christmas theme. The music that was sung and played between the women's entrances could build up to Christmas. Our Mary had to be young and not sophisticated in her manner. "Please Lord, help us!" we prayed. Right before our eyes was the answer to our prayer. One of the new believers in the Tabernacle church was in her eighth month of pregnancy. She really looked the part. With a giggle of acceptance, she received her instructions and her costume.

After presenting the program to a full auditorium in Madrid, we took it to Cordoba. The governor's palace auditorium became our meeting hall. The governor himself attended. He kissed my hand in congratulations. Wow! Several other occasions gave us full assurance that God blessed all the work, all the prayer, and all the rehearsals. Two teenage girls accepted the Lord in one of the programs. Several women signed cards, committing themselves to more consistent Bible reading.

How I loved ministering with the women of Spain in their (our) Union.

# 68 AT THE SOUND OF THE SIREN, PRAY! (1978)

God is always available to receive emergency calls. Christ is enthroned at God's right hand today, ruling the world through His intercession and the intercession of believers. He never turns anyone away.

The Lord convinced Bill of this in Madrid several years ago. He began to assume responsibility to pray for those in emergencies. Whenever he heard the fire bells or the ambulance siren he stopped to pray for three things: that the people involved would have an opportunity to know salvation through Christ, that God's perfect will would be done in their bodies, and that those who attended them would be merciful and efficient.

Wesley L. Duewel states the requisites for one who is part of God's "S.O.S. Prayer Network:"

Be sure you are filled with the Spirit.

Develop a deep prayer life.

Develop a conversational relationship with the Lord.

Develop a listening ear.

Ask God to keep you alert each day.

Accept responsibility for any special prayer burdens.[1]

We had no idea that one day God would give us the privilege of knowing the answer to one of those prayers made at the sound of the siren. We were finishing our after-dinner coffee in Spain, early in 1978. A heart-shaking crash of automobiles thundered in the air. We rushed to the balcony and saw people running, heard sirens blasting, and we went to prayer. The accident was just a few blocks down our avenue.

At that time, we were still involved with the team in establishing the Tabernacle church. One Sunday, many months later, one of the new Christians brought his neighbors, a young family, to the morning service. The father, mother, and two teenage daughters all walked with slight limps and the girls had faint scars on their arms and neck. At the close of the service Bill and I greeted them. They said, "We'd like to know more about personal salvation that the pastor talked about today."

The following Saturday, Bill and I went to the family's apartment. Sandalio, the father, ushered us into the living room and immediately went into detail about the auto accident they had experienced several months before, just a few blocks from our apartment. We remembered the sirens, the rush of people, and our response to pray the "S.O.S." prayer.

Sandalio, choked with tears, said, "I was conscious when they pulled me out of the wreckage and I was able to cry to God to spare our lives. We weren't ready for heaven. I asked God to care for us and give us a chance to know Him and serve Him here. Now we sit here with you and ask that you show us how to be ready to meet God." While I wiped the tears away, Bill opened his Bible and led the four accident victims to the Lord.

Sandalio and his wife, Elsa, told us more about the ordeal—the many days of lingering between life and death, their worry about the girl's scars, and their concern for being ready to meet God during that time. That was the only opportunity we ever had to know specifically the results of an "S.O.S." prayer. Most of the time is for God alone to know.

Our task is just to respond to the sound of the siren. God always hears us when we pray.

When that "nudge" comes to our minds and hearts, let us remember: At The Sound of the Siren, PRAY!

---

[1.] Wesley L. Duewel's book Touch the World Through Prayer—Francis Asbury Press, pages 79 and 80. Used with Permission.

## 69 TO LOOK BEYOND THE EXTERIOR FACADE (1978)

How intriguing to look beyond the exterior facade of people and see the REAL person. When Byron Dealey, our missionary colleague in Madrid, organized a reception in a hotel exclusively for students of the Bible Correspondence Course, Bill and I served as his hosts/receptionists.

Eusebia's bewildered expression drew her to me. She was shy at first. "This is the first time I've ever spoken face to face with an evangelical."

"And what do you think about us?"

"Oh, you aren't weird at all! In fact, you are all very nice! I'm glad I've come to hear the explanation of the Bible passage and to hear the good music. I'm not so afraid anymore." When she left that night, happy with the promise of a personal visit from one of us, her new friends, along with the Word of God's love sown in her that day, her face portrayed her satisfaction.

Jose entered quickly, a bright smile on his round face. He exclaimed, "Oh, that is the Gil that signs the courses (referring to Ruben Gil, our Spanish partner). I've received three courses. What a surprise to find that the Gil that signs the courses is the same Gil who sits near me in the Humanities class at the University along with Queen Sophia. What a discovery!" I thought his face was going to ache with all that smiling. I discovered that the smiles covered an aching heart, disappointed over the empty form of religiosity of his peers and the hypocrisy of the religion professors. His mask was bright, but there was heaviness in his heart.

Elisa was dressed in a drab gray coat, sizes too large for her, with no makeup, her hair drawn back in an elastic band which gave the impression of indifference. Far from it. She responded warmly to the caring attention from Berna Biddulph. She told us, "I read the correspondence course aloud to my teenage children every night. My husband has to read the verses. Then we all figure out the answers." We encouraged her to keep talking.

"We've been doing the courses for about two years now. Just a couple of months ago, we went to the Gospel Church on our street since we live on the far south side of the city. We're about ready to publicly confess our faith in the Lord Jesus."

Carmen was the most elegant woman in the group. Her dark-tinted glasses almost camouflaged her wistful eyes. She cautiously avoided revealing any details about her personal life or any of her ideas. As she was leaving I spoke to her a second time, but she wouldn't arrange any future meeting. She said, "I'll keep on with the course. I'm beginning to understand some things about myself as I read the Bible." Her sophisticated façade evidently covered a fearful soul. I prayed for her that as she read, perfect love would cast out her fear.

Joaquin's cordial affability didn't cover up anything at all. He enthusiastically shared, "I work in Albacete, 200 miles away, but I come back home to Madrid almost every weekend. Down there I attended a Crusade meeting and was converted to faith in Christ."

Byron asked, "Has that decision made a difference in your life?"

"You can be sure! My friends are sarcastic with me though, and my wife still opposes the Gospel but I'm learning patience. The course has helped me to trust the promises of God."

The most colorful person was Pepe. Flamboyant clothes, a frizzy hairdo, a wide pocketwatch chain, and slouching posture all added up. It was easy to see that he was a conformist to the crowd. He and Bill talked in the corner. Well, either Jesus and Christianity, or Marxism, I don't know which will win out. I'm not convinced about this Bible course. Maybe you're a bunch of phonies." He wouldn't let Bill get behind his "wall" and neither would he make an appointment for a personal conversation at a later date. He did however, sign up to continue the course.

Angela's placid countenance proved that she had already entered into "rest for her soul". She was the eldest attendee who immediately identified herself as a believer, declaring that she had come to faith in the

Lord through the course. She looked right in to my eyes, her dark blue eyes sparkling with joy. "Tell me about the Tabernacle. Maybe my son will take me there sometime. Imagine our joy when Angela arrived at the Evangelical Tabernacle a couple of weeks later, hardly missing a Sunday service from then on. Her baptism was a great celebration. Bill still has three elegant handkerchiefs in his drawer that she embroidered with his initials.

Dolores talked loudly, apparently sure of everything she said. It was easy to see beyond her mask though to a highly emotional, deeply hurt girl, who contrary to appearances was terribly unsure of her own worth. "I hardly know how to obey God," she confided. "I don't even know how to find the Bible references for the course. I spend half the time looking for the verse." Many weeks later, she allowed the Holy Spirit to get through to the real Dolores. What a change it made in her life.

Looks CAN be deceiving as the popular saying goes! At the reception, we were reminded again that evangelism cannot be impersonal. Christ through His Spirit guides us to reach the real person inside.

## 70 SINGLE-MINDED OBEDIENCE (1978)

Before going to Motril to be part of the church-planting team with Christian and Charo Giordano, Bill Eddy, and Judith Buchanan, we noticed that church leaders were being made more aware than ever before that single-minded obedience was the primary requisite for serving in the church. It encouraged us to see them take the Lordship of Jesus Christ seriously, willing to pay the price for doing whatever was necessary to obey and fulfill God's Great Commission.

One of the many leaders for whom we feel great affection and esteem is Angel Duran. He had been a contact in the correspondence course and telephone ministry so Bill, in his routine of follow-up calls, went across the city to visit him. Bill was feeling frustrated and discouraged because so many names and addresses he attempted to follow up on were false. Upon arriving at Angel's the apartment his mother informed Bill that he would not return for an hour or two. My patient Bill sat down to wait as he "entertained" the mother with stories of the Bible and his own experience of faith in the Lord.

When Angel arrived, he and Bill had a very significant conversation. Angel wanted to obey the Lord at any cost. Our Madrid Tabernacle was very far away. It was not feasible for Angel to travel on the bus and subway to the extreme other side of the city, so he got well established in a church near his home.

Almost ten years later, while we were in Indiana, we received a phone message to call Angel Duran in New England. What a surprise to hear from him again. We were to learn that Angel had come to the U.S. to study, had married, and now wanted to return to Madrid to serve the

Lord. We were overjoyed to welcome him and his lovely wife, Laura, into our family of OMS workers.

Bill would often remark to me his joy upon having carried through on that follow-up visit across town so many years before!

# 71 GLOOMY DAY CALLS (1979)

The MENSAFONO (recorded phone message) always received more calls on wet, rainy days. People were in a low mood on gloomy days and apparently got more serious about their spiritual condition. Every morning, I was responsible for changing the two-minute message on the recorded tape so that people who called in would have a fresh Gospel thought. Bill went out to visit some of those who had called, accompanied by Jose Luis, a madrile (inhabitant of Madrid) who had recently been baptized. Jose Luis, who recorded the messages that I had written, was interested in the outreach of the project. They returned to the office with the news that the first fellow they visited had received the flyer announcing the Mensafono two years before in the subway station and had just now decided to call. His dabbling in eastern religious philosophies had not satisfied his heart.

The next Sunday evening, Bill and I visited Ana, a fifty-six year old widow whose dog met us at the door. He was a Labrador with a big bark, bad breath, and a horrible manner of wanting to sit on my lap. Evidently he thought he was a Pekingese! His mistress, lonely and grumpy on that rainy day, cautiously told of her disillusionment with religious people. She had called the Mensafono after seeing our advertisement in the newspaper. As our friendship developed, I had to surrender to the Lord my disturbing feelings of jealousy. When she came into the church she looked over the congregation and having spotted Bill, went directly to sit beside him. (I often was beside the organ before singing.) When we took her home on rainy days or when she was especially depressed, she would boldly open the front car door and sit in the front seat! Despite all of that, when she publicly professed salvation in Jesus I was grateful!

## 72 I WAS THE ONLY WOMAN (1981)

How does one share a blessed, exploding heart in a few words? A group of twelve evangelists met at the Decision offices at Billy Graham Association and talked about choosing a woman to serve as Prayer Chairman to meet with the new committee they had formed. They agreed they must pray more regarding which of the two women they had suggested would be chosen. When they returned to vote the next week, each man put his voting slip into the hat. That week, I received a phone call from Antonio Pardo who said, "We voted unanimously to ask you to serve on the Evangelists Committee."

I was not free to say "yes" immediately. I had to consult with my husband and with our church planting team in Motril of southern Spain. Surprisingly, everyone gave a hearty vote of confidence and said, "Go with it!".

Much paperwork, travel promotion, and consistent prayer prepared the way for the First Conference of Evangelists in Spain. It is difficult to state which participation or activity of the Conference was the most outstanding. Perhaps it was the prayer emphasis. The prayer vigil will not be erased easily from my memory. There were three one hour periods of personal, almost silent confession, except for an occasional sob or sigh. In periods of confession for the sins of a nation and following the example of the prophets of old, we spoke of sin, including even the horrible Inquisition when so many Jews and evangelical believers were burned at the stake, killed by the sword, or beaten to death. In times of intercession for the unreached, when the overwhelming surge of voices lifted all at once like a murmuring stream, we were emphatically aware of 2 Chronicles 7:14—

> *"If my people, which are called by my name, shall humble themselves, and pray, and seek my face, and turn from their wicked ways; then will I hear from Heaven, and will forgive their sin, and will heal their land."*

Before anybody was stirring, the men of the committee and I gathered downstairs to pray each morning. As I walked from my room, I noticed the eye catching posters in the hallway and in the Prayer Chapel and remembered my dilemna about them. I had been very concerned to have them done well, which meant I was not the artist for the job. Besides, I had so much to do in the new church with the children and with mission responsibilities, I couldn't find a minute for them. I didn't want to spend much money for someone to do them for our budget was limited. Bill and I prayed specifically about that as one should do in any situation!

Five days before the Conference the posters were still not done. A stranger came into our church prayer meeting. He had seen our sign at the entrance of the city as he was hitch-hiking back to his hometown. God was dealing with him. He told us he had run away from the Lord, turning his back on the Gospel, but now he confessed his need for prayer. Bill and Christian Giordano, our pastor, prayed with him and after his testimony of victory, they helped him find an inexpensive motel since none of us had any extra beds at that time. (The Giordanos were living with us while their apartment was being renovated.) The next morning, the stranger said to me, "I notice you have a pile of poster board and paints. Do you work in sign painting?"

"Oh, no," I chuckled. "This is material to make posters for our Conference of Evangelists that takes place next week in Madrid."

"I'll do them for you. Where is the list of phrases you want on the posters? Do you have any particular colors? Show me where to work."

The posters were better than anyone had hoped. Our new friend was a professional! After the conference, I used the posters over and over again.

# 73. MY DARLING'S ACCIDENT (1982)

Even though the Lord has been very kind to give us children to love and nourish wherever we served, our grandchildren, Jana, Andy, and Raquel, take first place in our hearts. One hot, sultry afternoon, while making cookies for the Joyful Hour children, I answered the phone in a random manner. Immediately, I snapped to attention. It was our son Bill and his wife to report a very sad incident in our first grandchild's life. The previous day, May 6th, Jana Elisabeth went into the bathroom to get into the tub. She turned on the hot water and put her foot under the faucet to test the temperature. It was much too hot. The shock of it caused her to faint into the tub. The hot water poured over her neck and shoulders, burning her back, neck and shoulders. Her right hand and arm were very seriously burned. Bill said, "Jana's little brother was a real hero for he ran to get Mommy in the kitchen right away. Thank God for his concerned reaction!"

Her Mom was quick to grab a sheet and wrap Jana in its cold, wet folds. Bill was at the Olivet College library nearby from which he raced home to take his little girl to the hospital. A long hospital stay for burn care with subsequent grafts took up much of their time after that.

My husband and I have not been prone to leave the field for family happenings so we prayed much and wrote often. Now, looking back, how I wish I had just left everything in Motril and rushed to my darling's side. I have always called Jana Elisabeth "darling" for she is loved dearly. Why, then, didn't my love for her push me into securing a plane ticket? It was a long time before I could think about those days without feeling ugly guilt. Her mother wrote, "Thank God for His peace in times of heartache. Jana is recovering from skin grafts on both shoulders. Her hand has healed on its own. We praise God for helping Jana to cope with her pain and the 'why's' of it all."

# 74 TWO AND A HALF YEARS OF WITNESS AND FRIENDSHIP (1982)

Bill met Paco on a street corner in Motril. As is Bill's custom, he enjoyed conversation with the young, bearded sculptor who told Bill about his work, his likes and his dislikes. "Oh, I've been making images for the churches around here. I don't get much money for my labor though. I love kids so I like to whittle little things for them."

After a few minutes Paco was restless to move on. Bill added Paco to his prayer list. Over a period of more than two years, Bill's friendship with the melancholic artist developed slowly. Paco was wary of commitment. After all, he thought, Bill was a heretic! Paco and Bill would chat four or five minutes on the street, then Paco would get nervous and move on. Bill witnessed to his faith in Christ, but Paco gave no response.

A couple of times, Paco stepped inside our church, stood by the door glancing around cautiously. After five or six minutes he always slipped out. Then Bill invited him to view a movie that dramatically portrayed the second coming of Christ. Paco remained seated for the entire film. The pastor gave a clear invitation to accept the Lord. A couple of teenagers went forward to pray, but Paco remained in his seat.

Bill and I went home, played "Uno" with our neighbor girls, and then went to bed. Bill always sleeps very soundly and rarely hears anything at all. The phone rang at two-thirty in the morning so of course I, the light sleeper, answered after the first ring. "Hello," a voice spoke, "This is Paco. I've been walking the streets, going from tavern to tavern. I'm not drunk," he assured me. "I need to see Guillermo (Bill)."

"What hour do you want to come tomorrow?" I asked.

"Oh, I need to see him right now!" he insisted.

Bill answered his knock and the two went into the living room. I stayed back in the kitchen praying and dozing now and then. Around two hours later, they were on their knees at the coffee table. Paco acknowledged his sin, accepted Jesus as his Savior, and became our brother in Christ.

# 75 COFFEE WITH FRIENDS (1982)

Tears choked me. I gripped Bill's hand, struggling with my reactions to the solemn drama before us. Three hundred and fifty women, each with a lighted candle, moved by us in rows of six persons. Nine (only nine) seemingly indifferent men shuffled among them. Thirty preteen girls followed, dressed in black gowns with lace mantillas, caught up with elaborate combs.

Many spectators were kneeling before a large wooden platform shouldered by forty young men. The statue of the Virgin of Sorrows, robed in black and blue velvet, encrusted with sequins and gold beads, stood erect on the platform. Across her outstretched arms lay the bare, bloody body of a crucified Jesus. The city band blared out a mournful dirge. At the street corner four skyrockets bombarded the night sky with magnificent colors.

For some, the parade seemed to be a social gathering, but most people appeared to be moved. "¡Viva la Virgen! ¡Viva la Virgen!" (Long live the Virgin!) Their chant reverberated in my ears and I had to cry. It is the only way to God the Spaniards in our new city, Motril, had ever known. They were not aware that Jesus Christ is the Way, the Truth, and the Life. We longed to have them know that. We knew that the people who marched in religious processions and fingered their prayer beads every morning would not be coming to our church services.

As I looked back on that period of our ministry in Motril, in the province of Granada, I am sure we were right in wanting to relate to people where they were. Confidence develops between persons who spend time together. That happens when friendships are formed. Tracts were appropriate at times, a favorite of Bill's who seemed to use them more than anyone else on our team, but they were not keys to open the door to trust and familiarity. The Lord gave some fruit from the exhortation in preaching and the well-planned outdoor campaigns, but the people of Motril had no history of "evangelical" activity to understand coming to the church of the "heretic" to find Christ. Church services themselves did not establish the friendship necessary for trust. The people rarely came to a service without first having a relationship with one of us on the team.

Naturally, there were some who said "no" to our attempts at conversation. Others were slow, very slow to respond. That didn't mean that we rejected them. We wanted to be friends. Let me give you some examples.

Rosa lived on the same third floor of our apartment building. I followed the Motril custom of leaving our front door open in the morning while dusting and preparing the midday meal. Rosa and I often chatted at the door. Sometimes the dialogue ended with a time over coffee cups at my kitchen table or hers. I joined her in doing the daily marketing, although I have always preferred to get the groceries only once or twice a week. Her daughters became my friends with the consequence of a messy kitchen when they concocted strange fruit salads or flipped hotcakes. Her husband came home inebriated very often. In one of those times he spat at me, "You foreigner! You may speak our language well, but you'll never be one of us! We don't want you here." Rosa vehemently disagreed with him!

Four months after our first coffee cup chat, Rosa walked through my open door into our living room as she announced to me, "I want the kind of personal faith you have. You have to show me how to reach God like you do."

Emma smiled shyly when I greeted her in the open market. I knew she lived on our street. Eventually our relationship reached the "cup of coffee" stage in the corner snack bar with our full market baskets at our feet. One morning, she lingered at the table and said, "Lois, I realize you have some kind of special friendship with God. I'd like to have that, too, but I'm so afraid to change my religion. Yet, I need that serenity of spirit you have."

Days stretched into weeks. I didn't bother to count the cups of coffee. One afternoon, I answered a brisk knock on our door. Emma stood there, her eyes filled with tears. "Pray with me. My husband, Paco has beaten me again. The little girls were dreadfully rambunctious this morning and I shouted like an animal. I broke my pressure cooker, too!" In her desperation she came to me. I took her to my Lord.

Emma and Rosa stopped participating in the processions. They launched new lives of security for their souls because of their saving faith in Jesus, their Lord and Savior.

I STILL like conversation over coffee!

# 76 A TEST OF LOVE (1982)

Antonio's teeth were GREEN! He had NEVER used a toothbrush in all his eight years of life. I gave him a bright yellow one but he informed me with a big green smile, "I used it to wash the tires of my little sisters tricycle." He was shy, especially around adults. When I talked to him, he hung his head as he shuffled his feet around nervously. Antonio attended the Saturday afternoon "JOY" children's Bible club which is part of the church planting efforts in Motril. I really wanted Antonio to be won to the Lord. He had already won my heart.

Now I'm not against chewing bubble gum—in its place. My helper clown stood at the door with the trash can to encourage the kids to deposit their gum in the can as they marched into the "clubroom". Some deposited their "wad", but most didn't. Then, just as the singing and the contests were over when I concentrated on the really important time of the hour—the Bible lesson—the boys and girls (sometime as many as 130 of them) began to blow their bubbles! It was most disconcerting.

They interpreted my exhortations and pleas regarding the trash can as my disapproval of gum. It is my custom that when I have a problem to share it with my husband. I didn't have to this time because Bill was always in the Joy Club. He knew my dilemma. We prayed about it together. God gave us a solution. The next Saturday, we announced the upcoming Bubble Blowing Contest. Three different age divisions would compete. Excitement mounted, and on the appointed day the "jawbreakers" were distributed at the entrance door. The judges were in their seats; the children noisily took their places in their sections. I observed with amusement the moving jaws, the bright eyes, and the "I dare you to beat me" expressions. Now the gum was just right for making bubbles. The fanfare blared and the room suddenly blossomed with gum balloons. Unfortunately, some of those bubbles went awry ending up in hair and eyelashes! Antonio was one of the winners. He joyfully received his prize. The clown then passed the trash can so the bubblegum could be disposed of. This time the children complied. Then we were able to settle down for a good time of learning God's Word.

Several children, including Antonio, stayed after the club meeting to help put things away and sweep up the floor. As soon as I sat down with a weary sigh and put my feet up on a stool, Antonio climbed on my lap. No more shyness! He was elated over winning a prize and I was happy to listen attentively to his chatter. When he said, "Abre la boca," or "Open your mouth.", without even thinking, I did. Without warning, in he popped the gum he had hidden in his jaw. Yes, gum from the gypsy boy with green teeth! Displaying a magnanimous grin, Antonio then announced, "Es tu regalo. Te quiero." (It's your gift. I love you.)

I didn't spit it out. Someone called it a "sure test of your love—to chew gum from the child who had never used a toothbrush." For me, it was sure evidence of GOD'S LOVE!

Months after the gum episode, Antonio's mother became one of the first gypsy believers in Motril, Spain. She and her family are now part of the gypsy congregation there.

# 77 LATE NIGHT VISITORS (1983)

How many cups of coffee or sugar cookies must a missionary serve before the recipient yields to the claims of Christ? I lost count with Jose Luis, the electrician. He accepted the first cup of coffee with a big grin when he came with a satchel of tools to work in our apartment. He left munching on a cookie. Thereafter, about every two weeks, he showed up at our door between ten and eleven at night. He was a personable fellow, easy to talk to and attractive to look at. Bill always invited him to sit and chat awhile. Jose Luis hesitated to acknowledge the divinity of Jesus. Bill responded with biblical phrases. I fulfilled my hostess role by serving hot coffee and ham sandwiches or cookies.

"Give me some real proof," Jose Luis demanded.

Bill related his joy and assurance of salvation. Jose Luis then stated, "I doubt any intellectual would agree to your narration of the virgin birth."

Several cups of coffee later, Jose Luis brought his friend, Andres, to meet us. I imagine that Andres came to fortify our new friend's arguments. Bill gave them each a copy of Josh McDowell's book, <u>Evidence That Demands a Verdict</u>. Slowly, oh so slowly, the two young men began to look up the Bible verses referred to in the book along with others that Bill suggested. Many cups of coffee during the fifty weeks that followed cemented our friendship as well as their confidence in our testimony. They dropped their masks of skepticism when Christian Giordano, our partner/pastor of the Motril church, confronted them. Others of the congregation added their testimonies as they prayed for the young men.

Today, both of them are leading laymen in the church, feeling responsible that the congregation holds to sound biblical doctrine.

# 78 THE GYPSY BEGGAR GIRL (1983)

Juana had the face of a Baroque painter's Madonna. She stood at my door, wide brown eyes looking mournful with her thick, rather coarse hair drawn back in a flamboyant scarf. A chubby baby, wrapped in a stained piece of flannel, was cuddled next to her breast asleep. "Buenos dias," I said.

She straightened up and appealed to me, "Oh, madam, I need help. I'm all alone. I have no husband. I have no job. I have no money for food. Please give me some money."

"What is your name?"

"I am Juana."

"O.K., Juana," I said. "Come into my kitchen." Folks have scolded me for bringing an "unknown" into our home. I was to learn that Juana, a gypsy, was all of fourteen years old although she looked twenty. We talked while she ate the leftovers from lunch. Juana didn't know how to read. The father of her child still visited her once in a while. She said she thought she loved him and that maybe just maybe, he'd marry her someday.

"If you knew how to read you could get a job in the open market, Juana, and then you wouldn't have to beg everyday."

"Yes, I know. But I can't afford to pay for classes. My mother is so angry with me I don't think she'd watch little Carlitos while I go to class anyway. I'll just do like others do, hope that good people will be merciful to me."

"I have an idea," I smiled and continued. "You come here two or three times a week and I'll teach you how to read. You bring Carlitos. I like babies. He won't bother us."

So began a new schedule for Juana and me. While teaching her to read and write, the Gospel of the Lord Jesus Christ was worked in. It wasn't easy I must say. She was rarely on time. I had to teach her about body cleanliness along with the reading lessons. After the first sessions, I would find that some little things in the kitchen were no longer in their place! Eventually that changed.

Juana's victory arrived. Instead of begging, she was working. Instead of bickering and fighting with her mother, she was reconciled to her family. Instead of being afraid of dying, she was assured of the mercy of God and her salvation through Jesus Christ.

# 79 JOSE WAS CHANGED (1983)

"Jose, how about giving me your socks to launder? You've worn these five days now. You do have another pair, don't you?" That was one of the first ideas I planted in Jose's mind about cleanliness. He had come to our house to stay a while because his father, in a drunken rage, had expelled him from the home. Jose had given his father many reasons for anger because of his wild behavior with a gang during his teenage years.

Jose had been notified that his trial would come before the judge on December 15. He had waited more than two years for his case to be tried. Just a few weeks after he and his "buddies" had been caught for thievery and other bad conduct, he and a couple of his companions attended the opening film rallies that initiated the OMS ministry in Motril, Granada. The first night, they sat on the front row, passing their wine bottle from one to another as they heckled the California Quartet as they sang. The second night, they brought whiskey intending to stir up lots more trouble. The team members from Madrid intercepted their malicious plans. Surprisingly, the fellows returned the next night. Jose was the only one who attended with any regularity. When the final invitation was given one evening he slowly rose from his seat and slouched before the evangelist. God knew his heart. Jose's apparent nonchalance didn't fool the Lord. Jose, hungry in his heart for peace, prayed in repentance.

A clean heart and a right spirit don't always result in an immediate change in shower schedules or dress. The Holy Spirit took charge of the renovation with me acting as His agent. I even became Jose's hair stylist while he lived with us.

At his trial, Jose stood straight answering clearly to all the charges, admitting his guilt except for two occasions on which he said he was too drunk to recall what had happened. The lawyer requested leniency because of Jose's change in attitude, behavior, and even dress! The judge stated that the sentence would be declared on December 24th which meant a week of waiting.

The sentence?—100,000 peseta fine or one day in jail for each hundred pesetas not paid.

Our team continued praying for Jose's dilemma. Three days later a check from an anonymous friend in the amount of 80,000 pesetas was deposited in the church's account.

Only Bill and Christian Giordano, our pastor, knew who was the donor. Before long, the rest of the money was supplied as well.

Jose has remained a faithful attendee and helper in the church. When we purchased the old building whose interior needed renovation, Jose was one of the laborers. One of the little boys of the Bible club noticed Jose's sweaty torso. He remembered that I had talked about God being powerful, and quipped, "God has muscle, doesn't He? Powerful, but stronger than Jose!" I thought about God's greater than muscle power that had changed Jose's heart.

# 80 FLEXIBILITY: PLIABLE UNDER CHANGING CONDITIONS (1983)

Andalucia, Spain is a wonderful, wonderful place to celebrate Christmas. Early on Christmas Eve the young people dress up as shepherds and wise men then walk from house to house singing. We added our voices to theirs. During the whole season, our house was the scene of teas, suppers, special get togethers and the Christmas Eve dinner was to be the highlight of our entertaining experience. We had very special guests, Gordon and Elida Barnett, from Madrid. We had also invited our neighbors, all six of them, and Tonio a new teenage believer with his family of thirteen. The kitchen stove and counters were full to overflowing. I didn't feel rushed, though Just excited.

I was taking a little rest, enjoying a glass of juice, talking with our guests from Madrid, while listening to their gift cassette of Christmas carols. The doorbell rang. Thirteen-year-old Tonio came into the room with a long face. "I'm sorry," he apologized. "Mama says we can't come to your house. She's embarrassed because our Papa won't come. He's drunk." Well, we couldn't let that family have a supperless Christmas Eve. They had never really celebrated, not ever. So, I took my large tray down from the top shelf filling it with a dish of rice with vegetables, a platter of baked chicken, a plate of avocado salad, a loaf of cheese bread, and a huge and I mean HUGE plate of cookies and candy.

Tonio could hardly manage it.

We took apart one of the makeshift tables which were planks over sawhorses to revise our plans for the reduced number for our celebration. An hour later, about ten minutes before we were all ready to sit down, the doorbell rang again. Surprise!!! There stood Tonio, all scrubbed and smiling. Behind him beamed ten members of his family. The food he had taken home had looked and tasted so enticing that most of them decided to overrule their mother's decision.

While Elida entertained them with games and conversation, Bill ran out to the nearby rotisserie for chicken. Thankfully it was still open. I buzzed around the kitchen making up whatever I could with what I had on hand. Instead of putting up the other table we changed the serving plan. We ate buffet style. The little ones preferred sitting on the floor anyway. What a good time we all had, literally "licking the platters clean."

Later, during dishwashing and tidying, I heard Bill chuckle as he repeated one of my pet phrases, "Blessed are the flexible."

"What's that you said, dear?"

"You're getting pretty good at being pliable, flexible, Lois."

"You mean I haven't snapped yet? *I've just been stretched!*"

# 81 MY MOTRIL PALS (1984)

My sweet relationship with the boys and girls of the Saturday afternoon Bible Club enriched my life. They kept me from getting old! One afternoon, five giggling children knocked on our door just after Bill left to take the Men for Missions Crusade team to the airport. The kids were all talking at once. They held one big box tied with blue and red used ribbons and four little gifts wrapped in butcher paper, tied with brown string. The drawing on the big box amused me—two people hugging each other in the middle of a crooked heart.

The boys and girls surrounded me with much laughter and joking as I opened the gifts, wishing Bill was there to share the fun. It wasn't anyone's birthday nor our anniversary, just an occasion of celebrating love. One gift was a little, rather bedraggled plant. On the unevenly painted pot was a sweet message in tilted letters: "Luis ama a Loida" (Luis loves Lois). Luis was eleven years old. The other package held a macramé plant hanger. I already had four hangers, but I knew I would have to hang the new one, too. The next gift was a soccer emblem "to sew on my jeans." Rosita said. I had no blue jeans. The fourth box held a bell, a baby rattle for my kitty, and a day old donut for me.

The big box was a darling house for Gigi, the kitty. Her name was painted above the door in streaky watercolors. Tape reinforced the lopsided roof. The windows were all different shapes and sizes. What time they must have spent on these loving declarations of affection. My heart was full to the brim with thankfulness for their darling gifts.

After forcing Gigi to stay in her new house, taking a photo of the kids, and handing out cookies all around I "shoo'ed" them off to home and went to bed, feeling cherished, feeling happy, feeling tired.

## 82 A CATERPILLAR OPENED THE WAY (1985)

There was no specific formula that works for every church planting situation. One congregation was formed with new believers from the open air meetings and door to door visitations. Another church was established through contacts made from the Bible correspondence course. The church in southern Spain was initiated with a film campaign held in an open stadium. A church in Guayaquil, Ecuador got its start through a cottage meeting and personal witnessing. Another church in Guayaquil developed from a children's Bible class in the outskirts of the city. In fact, it took the name of the Bible Study group called "Noah's Ark"!

After the four years of challenge in Motril, God made us part of a church planting team in Pilar neighborhood in northwest Madrid. We prayed along with our companions, Miguel and Esther Fernandez, Clive and Angela Harffy, and Scott and Kathy Murphy, that God would give an innovative activity to call attention to the people of the area. God gave the answer! A large vacant lot that was only dirt beckoned to us. Children played there in the late afternoon when there was refreshing shade. The town council gave permission to OMS to use it for eight days. The transportation department *gave* us the iron "barriers" to fence it off. The Pocket Testament League in Barcelona loaned us their steel and wood platform, 430 chairs, placards, and a backdrop scenery for a "crusade" to feature children's rallies in the afternoon and films in the late evening. The Madrid Tabernacle loaned us the sound system and more folding chairs. There was an advantage to my being the older woman on the team. Our companions insisted that I *not* work on putting up the platform or setting up the chairs. Even so, Kathy and I were exhausted after going up and down the main streets putting 120 placards in store windows and snack bars. She made the remark, "I didn't imagine you had so much vigor!"

The kids received their entry "tickets" on the street when the CATERPILLAR announced the special event. "Caterpillar?" you ask. Esther made a long, wide, high wormlike creature out of green muslin, yellow taffeta and nine steel hoops. The catepillar's big, round face had lopsided eyes and a lolling, bumpy tongue. Ten helpers marched inside the hot tent of the caterpillar with the first one carrying the cassette that blared out the bouncy music. Esther led the "procession" as Bill and I ran hither and yon giving out the tickets for the rallies. Three days before the event took place, Bill drove the van up and down the streets of the neighborhood with two exuberant clowns perched on the roof, hilariously calling attention to their announcement.

The first day, the clamoring children waited noisily as the rally was delayed 45 minutes due to complications with the sound system. By the time I collected their tickets, their sweaty hands had almost mutilated the cheap cardboard.

I wonder if I can adequately describe that first day. 480 squirmy kids sat inside on the chairs while about 100 more leaned on the barrier railings outside. Behind them stood 250 adults, looking on. Above us, in all the apartment buildings, the windows and balconies were filled with curious faces. Wow! The kids loved the music quickly learning the Gospel choruses. They listened almost in a trance as the Bible story was acted out on the stage. When the clowns cavorted in silly antics the kids giggled contagiously. I was helping to keep order. During the first song, two eggs splattered all over my left front side. Later, a squishy tomato stained my skirt. Somebody had a mean thrust. I was glad it was me and not the other women of the team who were young and had not ever been attacked like that. The first rally, nonetheless, was a success. The kids left saying, "We'll be back tomorrow."

The second day was a bit different. Just minutes before the first choruses, Miguel and Clive had to stop a horrible fight when rival gang members pulled out their switchblades. 530 children crowded onto the chairs and sat down in the dirt at the front. I counted 200 adults standing outside the barriers. A woman with whom I had spoken the previous day shouted out crude epithets and a bystander swatted her on her backside which started a brawl. A young man then hollered, "Hey, you stupid old woman, your daughter is ugly and indecent." That only added to the woman's strident anger. Whew!

Angela overheard a group of men whispering about destroying the scenery. At the close of the program, our men folded the backdrop as small as possible for a nine foot high fourteen foot wide backdrop and shoved it away underneath the platform. Despite that, the next afternoon we were dismayed to see that someone had used cigarettes to burn it. When the men lifted it to the steel frame, a gust of wind tore at it ripping it from top to bottom. That day's program was delayed about thirty minutes as a result. God had already provided for the mishap since Miguel and Clive had "just happened" to bring the old backdrop from Barcelona along with everything else. It wasn't as artistically precise, but the kids actually liked it better than the first because it was gaudily colorful!

Sunday was the day for costumes. They wore all kids of costumes—outlandish, creative, beautiful, humorous, and weird. Clive, dressed as a Bedouin, and the two clowns were the judges who gave four prizes. 140 costumed kids gave us their names and addresses for follow-up.

The films were good, but the projector was faulty. The first film night about seventy-five people walked out because of it, but they returned the next night. We couldn't start the movie until ten-thirty because the Spaniards had to finish their evening supper. At intermission time, at the changing of the reels, I presented the literature. On the outside I was smiling and apparently poised, but in actuality I was trembling and nervous on the inside. Guest evangelist, Fernando Vangioni, always gave a brief but powerful invitation. We were excited to have 121 signed cards from adults at the close of the campaign. Seven children were brave enough to go forward at the invitation to accept the Lord Jesus as Savior.

After all the "paraphernalia" of the campaign was folded up and returned, we moved to the New Life Center two blocks down the street. All those who signed cards, including the children with their parents were invited to the reception. Fourteen people came, only fourteen out of so many. But we were not discouraged. The following Sunday, when Miguel preached the first sermon in the Center, sixteen people sat in a companionable circle. It was a great beginning!

## 83 YOU'RE ANGELS SENT FROM GOD (1986)

City wide evangelistic campaigns were not a common, normal activity for the church those first years in Madrid, but by 1986 the scene had changed a bit. Fears and prejudices were diminished so that a Latin American evangelist could preach in a large auditorium. At the close of those meetings the committee distributed the cards that had been signed by seekers to the follow-up personnel.

One Monday evening, Angela Harffy and I, with our follow-up cards, approached an apartment building in a posh section of north Madrid. The downstairs entrance door was open. No doorman was there to question our reason for entering which was a near miracle. As we left the elevator on the fourth floor I noticed the door was ajar to the apartment we were to visit. I knocked and called out, "Doña Margot'. Immediately, a very attractive dark-haired woman opened the door.

"¿Sí?" she asked.

I answered with a smile, "My friend and I received your name as a person interested in knowing more about following the Lord Jesus and we would like to…"

"Come in, come in," she interrupted, "You're angels sent from God." We sat on her sofa surrounded by boxes and half-opened suitcases. Margot had just returned from Portugal. "Now, how are you going to help me walk with Jesus?" she asked assertively.

Our friendship developed rapidly. Our personalities "clicked" and she quickly accepted me as her mentor and discipler. Chris, her eight-year-old son, especially liked my food as well as the games of 'Uno' we played after dinner in our apartment. Margot devoured the Gospel of Mark but when we got to the book of Romans, some of those strong truths bothered my new friend. We prayed that she would not resist God's guidance. Her story touched my heart and we both dabbed at tear-filled eyes as she told me about herself.

"My Cuban parents gave me all the advantages possible. They taught me not to 'disgrace our family'. My school days were spent in the U.S. which is why I speak both English and Spanish easily. My Portuguese grandmother helped me to add still another language to my ability. After my studies, I met a handsome Mexican who swept me off my feet. Following a very elaborate wedding, he carried me off to Mexico City. I wasn't as religious there as I had been at home. Social events, prestige, directing my maids, gardener, and cook and then having a baby took all my attention. Lois, did you know that I'm a specialist in needlepoint? I even had a popular television show for needlepoint instruction which made me feel very important. After a while, our lifestyle and a growing tendency to infidelity ruined our marriage. I felt that I was a failure.

After the divorce, my little boy and I settled in the U.S. I thank God for the 700 Club TV program through which my heart was drawn to the Truth of the Gospel. Through it, I responded to the invitation to accept the Lord. For a time, I attended a Bible class where a wonderful, compassionate woman helped me trust God and not be afraid. The threats of my ex-husband to take our son to Mexico constantly frightened me. I couldn't bear the daily tension. So I came to Madrid. I have a wealthy aunt here who has helped me get situated. I'm teaching English to cover my expenses and my brother sends me money, too. Through this flight to Spain, my adaptation to a different culture and my fear over my son, I have grown cold in my attention to God. I need more and more of the Lord. Help me."

In addition to our times of prayer, conversation, dinners and church attendance together, Margot found joy in the praise meetings of the gypsies. At this writing there are probably about 20,000 gypsy Christians in Spain. Their meetings are characterized by loud, expressive singing, and frank, persuasive testimonies. Culminated by an evangelistic sermon, affirmed by almost deafening "Améns" and Hallelujahs," Margot loved that atmosphere.

When we reached chapter twelve in the study of the book of Romans, Margot surrendered to the will of God. She knew that by coming to

Spain she had purposely made it difficult for her ex-husband to have access to their son. She stood up, her jaw set, her eyes sparkling, and declared, "I've got to do what God requires me to do. I should go back to the U.S. Let's pray a lot about it."

Upon arrival in the States, her attentive brother showed her a new perspective in the working world helping her get established in the computer business, using her Portuguese and Spanish. Now our dear daughter in the Lord, Margot, lives in the U.S. I could not love her more if she were my own flesh and blood. She has taken her prominent place beside other women in my heart!

# 84 WITH A TOWEL AND WARM WATER (1986)

As president of the Madrid chapter of the Women's Union, I was responsible for guiding the board in decisions regarding programs of prayer, testimony, health and moral issues.

The women lovingly cooperated so beautifully that I was puzzled and surprised when I began to sense some jealousy and tension developing. What does one do in such a situation? Why, PRAY, of course! My concern that the Holy Spirit control our meetings took my attention day and night. It lay there in my heart as I went about other activities in the church and the mission.

One early morning while sitting in the living room looking out at the city lights, the Lord lighted my mind with an idea.

> *Please come to my house Thursday at ten a.m. for coffee and a different experience with the Lord. May I suggest that you not wear pantyhose?*

The women were accustomed to my creativity so they didn't question that strangely-worded invitation. My table was set with flowers and embroidered napkins but I only served an ample piece of coffee cake and coffee. No frills. Then we went to the living room and sat in a circle. I didn't assign their places, but as usual, the Lord had His way! The woman who had been most negatively vocal sat on my right. On the serving card to my left I had the following items: a large pitcher of warm water, a basin, a small pile of towels, and Kleenex. Then I opened the Bible and read John 13 where Jesus washed the disciples feet.

I asked the women to take off their shoes. I knelt before my sister on my right and held her right foot above the basin, dripping the warm water over it, and said, "Sister, I appreciate the gifts God has given you and how you have served so consistently with the Women of the Union. Thank you for being part of my life. I thank the Lord for you. I love you."

With that last phrase, Alicia grabbed a Kleenex to wipe away the tears. Then I washed her left foot and dried her feet. Around the circle, each woman took her turn with the basin and the towel. One woman stood and hugged another, almost tipping the basin of water. The strong and sincere love of reconciliation blessed us all. My prayer was answered through a basin and a towel!

At the next board meeting, when we had to plan the anniversary celebration, the smiles of appreciation glowed on their beautiful faces. Not a word of conflict, disagreement or criticism was uttered.

## 85 "LOIS, MEET JUAN!" (1987)

I had expended much energy in the Sevilla Women's Conference singing, speaking, counseling and praying. So on the train returning to Madrid I lay my head back. I didn't even bother to look out at the lovely, dusty green olive groves or the little villages tucked in the craggy hills. I just rested. Then as we got nearer to Madrid I began to dream. With every clickity-clack of the wheels my heart beat faster. I was feeling romantic, very sentimental.

Three days previously, when I left Madrid, I had said to Bill, "Don't take time to meet me at the station, Honey, 'cause I know you'll be involved in visitation. I'll take a taxi. It's not far." In the taxi, I planned my candlelight dinner thinking I'd use our new Mozart tape as a background. As my finger pushed our doorbell I was already smiling for my darling. He'd better be ready for a passionate kiss, I thought.

Bill opened the door wide, his sweet crooked smile welcoming me. At his side, almost leaning on him, was a bleary-eyed, rather unkempt fellow I'd never seen before. "Hi, Honey." Bill greeted me. He leaned forward to take my luggage. "I want you to meet

Juan. He's going to stay with us for a few days."

Well, that was that! No romantic dinner tonight!

Bill told me how he had been making visits, wanting to talk to people about their need for Jesus. "During three days of witness no one responded. This afternoon, going up the little hill toward home, feeling down in my spirit I prayed, 'Lord, give me someone that I can show Christ's love to.' Just then a man stepped out in front of traffic, weaving drunkenly. I drew him safely back to the curb. It was Juan. We sat on the bench and talked. His mother had told him to get out because she didn't want him in her house while he's so mean, drunken and filthy-mouthed. He has no money and no relatives nearby. So I've brought him to our apartment."

Juan stayed ten days following Bill around like a puppy. In fact, the only time Bill could escape him was when he went to the toilet or closed our bedroom door to be with me! I don't remember that we celebrated our time alone with a romantic dinner. I think we were too disappointed about Juan. During a period of nine months, Bill kept contact with him. We visited Juan's mother periodically. Because of her physical handicaps she could rarely leave the house for a worship service, but she came to love the Lord. Juan continued in his drunkenness, his vile-mouthed criticism and his unwillingness to come to Christ. Something deep, deep down in his unforgiving spirit drove him to hate.

Bill and I had a two month deputation ministry period in the British Isles. When we returned to Spain, Miguel, our colleague in church planting, gave us some shocking news. He said, "Juan is dead. He threw himself down to the street from his mother's ninth nfloor apartment. He told her he was going to do it in order to punish her. She tried hard to talk him out of it. As far as we know he never made his peace with God."

We wanted to be the Holy Spirit's assistants in giving Juan God's love, but Juan distorted that love. What a tragedy! Yet, his mother needed our availability and being involved in his life drew us to her. Though Juan was gone, she was right there in our neighborhood to nurture and affirm others in the Lord Jesus.

# 86 I TEARFULLY RETURNED TO MADRID (1987)

All seven of Mom's children stood around her hospital bed. Her pale face expressed her weakness and pain but her eyes smilingly glided from person to person. Bev, the youngest, in hushed whispers asked, "Mom, do you want to sing?" Her head nodded slightly. In muted tones we sang: *"This is my story, this is my song Praising my Savior..."*

Her feeble alto joined us on the short closing phrase, "All the day long." That was the favorite hymn of my "practically perfect," beloved mother.

I had been there in Florida almost twenty-five days, very sad for the occasion of Mom's approaching death, but elated to be with my two brothers and four sisters. We had been separated by many miles for so many years. The last brief time to be together had been in Charlotte's home in Parma Heights, Ohio for an afternoon picnic in 1973. The day following that sweet acappella harmony in Mom's room, I held her thin hand and thanked her for praying for Bill and me, especially thanking her for remembering my ministry to the women in Spain. She smiled warmly. Her raspy whisper made my heart beat harder, "Lois, honey, I want you to go back to Spain now."

"Mom, why on earth do you say that?"

"Because I know you're scheduled to participate in the Women's Retreat." She heaved a labored sigh. "Please go and keep your word. Please, please go back where you belong. That would make me very happy." In the following silence, I didn't feel uneasy. The Holy Spirit confirmed God's will in that quietness. I prayed again with Mom and then left to make the travel arrangements.

My brothers and sisters remained. I tearfully returned to Madrid, knowing that Mom's going was near. Five days later, in Madrid, my suitcase was ready by the front door, along with the song sheets and the handouts for the seminar. During those five days each time the phone rang I had thought it would be to tell me that Mom was gone. Just as I lifted my suitcase to leave, the phone rang again. Dad's voice communicated, "Lois, your mother is gone to be with her Lord. We'll have the funeral Saturday afternoon." His voice was strained and weak. I knew he'd had a tense time before the Lord, finally releasing Mom from her suffering.

Gordon and Elida Barnett, our friends from the Madrid Tabernacle, took me to the Retreat. They allowed me to be silent on the trip, giving me opportunity for composure. Oh, how God helped me in that Retreat! The poise and serenity He gave me to participate and care for my responsibility is indescribable. Many women commented, saying that my being there was a testimony to God's grace and provision. Amen to that! Of course they didn't see me thrown across my cot, crying and praying, after singing or speaking on the platform before those six hundred sisters in the Lord. They only saw my outward victory.

My mother was faithful to her Lord and to her family. I was constantly aware of her love for me. Mom was a precious, gentle, compassionate prayer warrior and leader of prayer groups. I never doubted her love. I never doubted her solicitous care for me. Dad found the most comfort with Nancy, the middle sister, who married Dr. Hal Kime. He said to me one day when I visited him later in Seminole, Florida, all alone, in the big house. "I think I'd prefer to die in Nancy's house in Arizona. That would be a good place. Yeah, that would be nice." Eventually that is just what happened a few months later.

# 87 MY TIMES ARE IN GOD'S HANDS (1987)

"There is a time for everything," Solomon wrote in Ecclesiastes, chapter three. "My times are in Your hands..."a phrase from Psalm 31. Over and over again, I am profoundly impressed that as Bill and I deposit everything into our Lord's hands, He controls the events.

Circumstances in God's providence delayed my needing cataract surgery. My eyesight became so poor that I accidentally put grated cheese in my iced tea and sugar on my spaghetti. So, the morning of the first cataract removal and lens implant, I was singing in my heart in St. Luke's Cataract and Laser Institute in Tarpon Springs, Florida. Thinking I was alone in the preparatory room, I began to sing aloud, softly to the Lord. The anesthetist remarked from behind my chair, "You're surely different. I don't think I've had a patient sing like that before." In the next room where they checked the vital signs, I sang softly again, this time a little numb in the head! The nurse, while taking my blood pressure and pulse, smiled at me, "You're different. Who are you? What do you do?"

She liked my response and confided in a choked voice, "God is calling me to be a foreign missionary, but my boyfriend says he can never do that. I'm miserable. I don't know what to do."

"When I go into surgery," I suggested, "why don't you go to the waiting room and talk to my husband. He has a gray goatee. He will probably be reading his Bible." Then we clasped hands and prayed together, sisters in the Lord. She waved as I went into the operating room as she headed out to find Bill.

Two days later, when it was time to remove the bandage, Michelle was at the door waiting for me. "What a radiant smile you have dear." I observed.

"Last night I broke off with my boyfriend and this morning I enrolled in the Night Bible Institute. I'm on my way!" I returned nine days later for the lens implant in the left eye. I left Bill in the waiting room talking seriously with a man experiencing his first cataract removal. For some reason, in God's timing, I had a long wait in the holding room. To my delight, Michelle came in. After she performed her duties, we held hands and prayed together. As soon as we finished, the man in the next chair spoke up. "You prayed in the same way a man talked to me out there in the waiting room."

Michelle answered, "We prayed like that because we know Jesus personally and know that He hears our prayers."

"Probably you'd like to know the Lord Jesus in a personal way, too." I added.

"Yes, yes I would," he said. "It's about time I get my heart right with God."

So there we were, Michelle and I, praying with the patient whom God had prepared in His timing, in His way, through Bill's witness in the waiting. Michelle made plans to go to Central America upon finishing her studies of the Bible. The gentleman patient and I appeared at the clinic the same hour the following Monday for the removal of our bandages. We shared as we waited. He told me that he went to church the previous day and that during the invitation time, he stood to his feet to give public witness of his clean heart. God honors those daily prayers in which we say, "Lord, my times are in Your hands. Take control. Use me for Your glory."

## 88 THE WRONG KIND OF SHOCK ABSORBERS (1988)

On December 2, 1988, Nora Suman could have been celebrating her birthday, but God gave her an assignment of loving concern. Bill was at the camp accompanying a drug addict who was "librándose del mono" (getting the "monkey" off his back—quitting the drug habit). Ten days with the tense, highly irritated young man was about all Bill could handle alone. He called for one of the believers from the city to help him. Nora, a sweet willing colleague, offered to take the helper out to the camp that night. There was no man available to do it. After delivering her passenger, she headed back to Madrid alone in a snowy mist at two o'clock in the morning. About twenty-five kilometers from the camp, still in the mountains, she hit a curve covered with ice. The car rolled over twice, down an embankment, and then skidded to an abrupt halt.

Nora told the story, "Grateful to be alive and right side up, I started the motor hoping to get back on the road. However, no matter what I did the car wouldn't move forward or backward. There was nothing I could do but work my way out of the car and climb up the embankment."

The air was biting cold. Nora's knee was swollen. The wind stung her face. She was afraid that the distant barking dog packs would attack. But God strengthened her as she walked the five kilometers in the darkness to the police station. Nora rode in the tow truck to the scene. When the driver turned his flashlight on the little car, he and Nora both gasped in amazement. The front tires rested on the very edge of a cliff! "Lady, there's got to be someone up in heaven watching over you!" he exclaimed. Nora quickly agreed.

The whole missionary team responded with overwhelming thanksgiving when Mic and Nora relayed what the mechanic in the garage discovered. "For some strange reason, your auto has shock absorbers normally used only on racing or cross-country vehicles. Those shocks saved your life and the car from severe damage."

Bill and I have often thanked God for the closely-knit relationship of sharing with the members of the OMS team wherever we have served. Fellow missionaries become family, relevantly illustrating Paul's words in 1 Corinthians 12:12a, 25b and 26, "For as the body is one…that the members should have the same care one for another and whether one member suffer, all the members suffer with it; or one member be honored, all the members rejoice with it."

## 89 A STEP INTO THE UNKNOWN (1989)

"Sergio, you're so sweet, I could just gobble you up!" The pre-schooler giggled as he ran into my arms. He was at our house often for he was the son of our partners in ministry, Miguel and Esther Fernandez. It wasn't possible for us to be with our own grandchildren so God gave us surrogate grandkids. (He also gave our grandchildren surrogate grandparents for which I thanked God.) I didn't appreciate the idea of leaving him or his little sister nor any of the other Spaniards who had invaded our hearts.

OMS wrote a very serious letter presenting a scary challenge to us. "Will you pray about going to Greece for us?" They proceeded to state the problems briefly, saying that our "testimony of integrity and faithfulness" qualified us for a delicate job. I set the letter aside with a chuckle expecting to answer at a later date along with other correspondence. I just knew that it was out of the question. We were too tuned in to the witness in Spain.

Have you been aware that God's way is perfect? We've always said that. In fact, we received a plaque for our twenty-fifth wedding anniversary with that phrase from Psalm 18 etched into the wood. It stared out at me every time I sat down at the desk. A couple of days later, Bill said in his inimitable, quiet way, "Dear, we have to pray about this and seriously consider a move." For several days, we prayed about it aloud in our devotional times together. During that time, Andrew Murray grabbed my attention in one of his paragraphs:

> *The faith that always thanks Him not for experiences, but for the promises on which it can rely, goes from strength to strength.*

I said, "I don't think I have the strength to leave Spain and go to such an unknown place like Greece." God convinced me otherwise. So, the day Bill declared, "I think we should cooperate with OMS in this matter and go to Greece," I nodded my head, grabbed my notebook and began to make my lists for preparation.

Knowing that it was God's will to go to the unknown was helpful when the tears came and my heart hurt at the thought of leaving my beloved Spaniards.

## Challenged

*Life stands ahead and beckons to me*
*To new paths yet untrod,*
*And asks the service of my hands*
*To work some task for God.*

*Life stands ahead and calls to me*
*To use my gifts of mind*
*To bless the sphere in which I move*
*With truths which I shall find.*

*Life stands ahead inviting me*
*To give my warmth of heart—*
*Man's spirit needs a healing touch*
*And kindness has its part.*

*Life, ah, Life, today I come*
*To meet you joyously,*
*And He who is the Lord of life*
*Shall walk along with me.*[1]

"He that findeth his life shall lose it: and he that loseth his life for my sake shall find it." Matthew 10:39.

With the challenge of that poetry engraved on my heart, I followed my husband to the most difficult assignment of our missionary career—to the land and culture of Socrates and Alexander the Great—to a country dominated by the Greek Orthodox Church.

---

[1] From a collection of poems by Phyllis Idle Johnson, "Splendor Where You Are", published by Zondervan Publishing House, 1958. Used by permission of her daughter, Myrna.

# GREECE
A land rich in Biblical and historical interest…

## 90 SHE THOUGHT I WAS KIDDING! (1989)

"Uh oh," I exclaimed to Bill. "I can't hem this dress. I have no thread this color. I'll just run down to the little shop around the corner and get some." The shop was in the home of an energetic Greek woman. I knocked, went in, smiled and said in my very best Greek, "Please, I'd like a spool of thread to match this swatch."

She rattled something so fast that I held up my hand and said with a smile, "Please, speak more slowly. I'm a foreigner and I don't understand when you talk fast." We were studying Greek in an accelerated course and even though my tongue surprisingly cooperated well with the learning of the phonetics, my ears were slow to grasp meaning to the rapidly spoken words.

Again, she spouted out a long sentence, raising her eyebrows and gesturing with her hands to emphasize her point. I smiled again and repeated, "Oh, please speak more slowly. I don't understand what you are saying. I'm new in Athens."

This time the woman frowned, pounded the counter and said, much more slowly, "What do you mean? How dare you try to kid me? Look at you. You're Greek. You speak Greek. Here is your thread!" She turned around and picked a spool from the shelf but it was obvious that she was very perturbed with me. When I told Bill about the incident he laughed and said, "She probably had a fight with her husband and took out her wrath on you! But, honey, you DO look Greek…and you sound sort of Greek!,

I guess I should just be thankful God graced me with a good ear for learning new languages even if it gets me in trouble!

# 91 HOPE FOR TOMORROW (1990)

God sent us to Greece on a difficult mission. Bill and I, along with our team of "youngsters", Tom and Chris Johnson along with Gary and Mary Burgin, were often overwhelmed with the sense of awareness that God was in control. We recognized that surrender to God's will takes the dread out of tomorrow. We all wanted to obey God in the matters of the field. We were sure that He assumed the responsibility for every future day.

Bill and I had great fun sharing our experiences and lessons learned from church planting in the previous years in Ecuador and Spain. Tom and Gary took many notes in preparation for their future. We gave them many photocopies of outlines and suggestions regarding personal evangelism and the initiation of a budding congregation. When we prayed together, inevitably the phrase "guide us about getting a new church started" came up in someone's supplication. We six adults, along with the children, made a precious family of communication. We had exciting plans for the two couples to continue the ministry by reaching out in the neighborhood where Tom and Chris lived.

The difficult decisions I had to make to put the field on order sometimes put a darkness in my feelings. One early morning God seem to whisper to me,

> "Beloved, do not try to get out of a dark place, except in God's time and in God's way. The time of trouble is meant to teach you lessons that you sorely need."

Just then a friend in Australia, not knowing my situation wrote, "Feelings come and feelings go, but feelings are deceiving, just hang onto God's Word dear sister, whatever your circumstance. It is not fickle!"

When Gary and Mary left the field, I wrote in my journal:

> Thy Lord, who sees the end from the beginning hath purposes for thee of love untold...
>
> Then place thy hand in His and follow fearless, till thou the riches of His grace behold.

The long trainride from our apartment to the Johnson apartment for prayer times and Sunday evening fellowship with the new believers fortified our faith, for we prayed going and coming. Occasionally, Bill went to the park or to the train station to talk with someone about the Lord, with his interpreter, young Andrew Johnson. One afternoon, he joined our prayer group with a big jubilant grin on his face. Andrew showed us the same happy face as he told of their witness to a young boy who listened very seriously to their narration of the love of Jesus for him. He prayed the sinner's prayer, took a couple of tracts, and left, turning to wave with a smile.

While we were praying, Chris answered the telephone. "Listen to me. Are you the people who gave my son that heretical literature? Well, if you ever approach him again I'll call the police. He is a minor. You have no legal right to proselytize. STAY AWAY FROM HIM!" The caller slammed down the receiver. Chris stood before us, her eyes wide with emotion. Her phone number was stamped on the literature so they had assumed she was involved.

Andrew spoke up, "We'll probably see the boy in heaven." However, this literal "wake-up call" made us aware of a potential problem. When Chris and Alecos, from the Bible Institute, gathered a few children in her living room for a children's Bible study each child had to present a signed permission slip from the parents in order to conform to the law.

Meanwhile, we comforted ourselves with the realization that Jesus Christ is no security against storms. He is the perfect security IN storms, however. He never promised us an "easy passage," but only a safe landing. The Holy Spirit would lead us through the storms of Greek laws and peoples' prejudices.

## 92 THE SONG FROM A MARBLE SLAB (1990)

I talked to Ken and Vicki, friends from the English school in Athens, and shared, "I'm so tired." Bill was in the U.S. representing the field in Missions Conferenes.

Ken and his family declared, "Saturday should be a rest day for you. No arguments! We're going to take you outside the city." What a delight to leave the heavily populated city and to get out into the hills as we walked in the refreshing breeze. We arrived at an amphitheater that had been used for orators in the time of Paul, the apostle. It was a natural "bowl" with seats of marble carved out of the hillside all around. Down in the center, the speaker could stand on the flat marble slab and be heard up to the farthest row, even if he whispered! What acoustics!

Ken said, "Go down there, Lois, and sing us a song. The kids will sit over there (indicating a seat halfway down the other side) and we'll stay up here." I felt silly and self-conscious. I rejected the idea. But he persisted and eventually persuaded me saying, "No one's down there. Go ahead. Make it a present to us."

"Well, I guess I should please them," I said to myself. I started down the steps thinking, "I'm in Greece so I'll sing How Great Thou Art in Greek." It was one of the few songs I knew by memory in Greek. Halfway down, I changed my mind, thinking it would be more considerate to sing in English for Ken and his British family. Just as I stepped onto the little slab and opened my mouth something strange happened. I began to sing in SPANISH! I sang part of it very softly, to test the acoustics, then increased my volume. I had a wonderful time singing. I then closed with the last chorus in English, singing with all my heart to the Lord.

The two children before me clapped, but to my surprise I heard applause from behind me. A group of over fifty people on the far side who had been listening to a guide, came toward me with big smiles. They were from Spain! They heard the hymn in their own language! I knew God did that. I stood there with them quite a while, explaining the song and my faith in the God of faithfulness. They all strolled away except for one young couple. They had more questions. They had joined the tour group for the Greece portion of the trip, but were on their way to Israel. They were working on doctorates in the music of the Sephardim or Spanish Jews. I offered to send them copies of thirty-three psalms with music notation that I had just received from an acquaintance who had been involved in archeological digs in Israel. The couple and I exchanged letters for almost a year. I was able in that time to give a clear witness of the Gospel. They used one of the psalms on the audiocassette I had recorded in Madrid four years later. I had hoped to visit them in their northern Spanish town, but it never worked out. I hope to see them in heaven!

# 93 A DIARY OF DISASTER (1990)

I wrote the following report to our OMS headquarters with tears and nausea washing over me as I relived the days of a disaster in Greece:

July 14th—Tom and Chris Johnson left Athens with three-year-old Evan and five-year-old Sarah along with four friends. They were going to Kalamos, an evangelical church camp for the evening program. Stephen, eleven years old, and Andrew, ten years old, the Johnson's oldest children, were there and would participate. At approximately 5:30 p.m., north of the city on the National Highway, the dreadful accident occurred.

The police detectives have not completed their investigation at this writing but made a statement, "An unknown driver, coming into Athens, was driving very, very fast and nicked a Honda Civic going in the same direction at about one hundred miles per hour. The first car sped away. The Honda jumped the median and headed for the Johnsons' Mitsubishi van traveling at the legal speed limit in the far right lane going north. All passengers were buckled into their safety belts. There were repeated skid marks. Tom Johnson, the driver, had nowhere to go and apparently braced himself against the steering wheel. Upon impact, the Honda was cut in half and the front half, with the engine, swung around and hit the side of the van."

That was the side where Chris and her friend, Maria, were sitting. The van tumbled over at least three times. Four other cars piled up behind. The young mechanic who drove the Honda and his unknown girl companion (no documents, perhaps a foreigner) were killed instantly and were quite mutilated.

None of the people in the pile-up of cars were killed, but several received internal injuries. Maria died immediately. Maria's son died, too, almost instantly. Her daughter, Elena, suffered bruising in her body and her left leg and knee cap were badly shattered and required immediate surgery. Giannos, the other passenger, suffered severe head damage.

Chris died within three hours of the crash. When she arrived at the hospital, she was smiling and speaking a bit. Her blood pressure was almost zero and her body was almost cut in half.

Sarah's left leg was badly broken, her head very bruised, her upper back had a couple of cracked disks and she breathed with difficulty. She was in severe shock. Evan was not moving. His face and head, too, were badly bruised. His right lung and kidneys were injured. He hardly complained, though. He didn't move his torso or his legs.

At first, it was thought that Tom was hemorrhaging in the brain. He was sedated because of his restless writhing in pain which was injurious to the many fractures. His face and head were a swollen mass of bruises, his eyes were swollen shut. He had cuts over all his body and three shattered fingers The left hand and wrist had multiple breaks. Both legs were fractured and shattered in several places. All who saw the van were shocked that Tom came out alive.

Fred and Sarah Raft, Chris' parents, had already returned to Greece as independent missionaries. Sarah went to the Children's Hospital immediately to care for the two grandchildren. As soon as others of us were notified, we stepped in. Hospital nursing staff is very limited in Greece and friends and family members are required to care for their loved ones.

July 15th—Many Greek believers went to prayer for all concerned because the accident was reported on national television. God provided many helpers for funeral arrangements, thus alleviating the Rafts in this sad experience.

July 16th—Stephen and Andrew returned from camp. When Grandma Raft told them about the disaster, they said with tears, "We know Mommy's with Jesus." Bill and Henrietta Johnson, Tom's parents arrived from Michigan and took over the responsibility of the boys.

July 17th—Tom and Chris would have celebrated their fourteenth wedding anniversary. Mary Burgin, Chris' younger sister, arrived in time for the funeral and God gave her beautiful ability to communicate strength to her parents.

It is impossible to list all the ways God's grace was evidenced during those days. Bob and Phyllis Erny came from Greenwood to extend their efficient helpfulness. Bob gave advice and encouragement while Phyllis gave nursing attention. I counted twelve men and women who took turns caring for the children along with the five men and women who cared for Tom.

By July 30th, Tom was out of the intensive care unit. The bones in his face were not knitting correctly though. Much of his body was in casts, but he was mentally clear, praise the Lord. He communicated with Sarah and Evan through a cassette tape message. They still had not been told of their loss because the psychologist suggested that their Aunt Mary tell them when the initial trauma was further behind them.

On July 31st, we saw God move mountains! The doctors released Sarah and Evan to fly on stretchers to Oregon with Mary Burgin and Sarah Raft. The most compassionate airline agent we've ever known had passed the scene of the accident. He had seen the vehicles and the bodies lying nearby. He told Mary and me, "I have two preschoolers like Sarah and Evan. I will do everything possible to make room for their stretchers."

Mary had gone to several other airlines before reaching KLM. What a considerate company! That agent remained in his office one day for two and a half hours on his personal time working on the case. He made over sixty telephone calls. Grant Nealis, our OMS "helper" in Greenwood, went all the way up to the first Vice President of American Airlines to persuade them to take the stretcher cases to Oregon from Chicago. Shriners' Hospital had not hesitated in accepting the children. Money was available for all expenses. I sold an apartment that OMS had owned for a long time in Athens.

Although some of that money had to go into a "restricted account," the rest was more than enough to cover travel costs. The CAT scans were free! Bill had been friendly with the father of the pathologist who demanded his daughter do her work without charge. I was spiritually blessed and impressed through the dealings with the U.S. Embassy people. The consular official, a young Christian, solicitously prayed for us. God gave me a competent Christian lawyer to help with the power of attorney and legal matters and gave advice about sales, etc. Maria, my beautiful, dedicated secretary interpreter, gave willingly, filling in the gaps through commitment.

August 3rd Tim flew on a stretcher via KLM to Chicago, then on American Airlines to Detroit to a hospital there. His parents and the older boys accompanied him.

Bill and I stayed on in Marousi, the northern neighborhood where the Johnsons had their apartment. Tom is very meticulous! I suppose accountants usually are. When he was finally able to communicate he asked me to make a list of EVERYTHING in the apartment because he couldn't remember what should be sold, given away, or packed for the U.S. I filled a few days with list making, twenty-six lists of their possessions. I'll leave it to your imagination the work involved in selling and packing up! I was overwhelmingly weary. One day I answered the telephone. The caller said, "I'd like to speak to Chris Johnson, please. She's been keeping some things for me."

"Oh, didn't you hear? Chris was killed in a terrible accident and was buried in the cemetery here in Athens."

"That is horrible, just horrible. I'm so sorry. How is her family? I'd like to pick up my suitcase." The caller replied.

After describing the accident and giving her the news on the condition of the other family members, I inquired, "What was your suitcase like? What color was it? How large was it?"

"It was a small, pale blue overnight bag. When I gave it to Chris a couple of years ago, she said she'd hold it for me until I returned from England."

I told her to come out to the house that very day. My heart was heavy and I wiped away the tears as I prayed to the Lord about my encounter with the owner of the suitcase. When I made the list of things, I noticed the unlocked bag with no name, making note of the contents, thinking that probably Chris had put them away for a special anniversary celebration. The bag had contained a new chiffon negligee set, silver slippers, a radio cassette player and some makeup. Since Tom had not marked them for keeping or selling I gave all but the radio cassette player to one of the girls at the Bible Institute who was planning her upcoming wedding. I sold the radio cassette player for about thirty dollars. I had to tell this woman all of that. She was disappointed and expressed the desire to be reimbursed. I gave her my personal check for two hundred dollars. She left shaking her head but not before we held hands while we prayed for Tom and his family.

I could end the whole experience of Greece with the phrase "to be continued." Though we had no missionaries in Greece, the influence of OMS was going to be carried on through the training of disciplers. Missiologists still say that Greece is probably the least likely place in Europe for the Gospel to prosper. That realization does not detract from the awareness of the urgency. Young Greeks responded to God's call with determined obedience. Through money received from the transfer of properties in Greece to another mission, a Christiana Johnson Memorial Scholarship Fund was established. Each year, a scholarship is provided for a worthy young person to study at the Greater Europe Mission Bible School where Dr. Robert Hill, an OMS "MK" is a member of the staff.

Chris was a fragile person with very strong motivation and multiple gifts for ministry. She was not capable of pretense and made no attempts to cover up her own weaknesses. Our lives are like a series of mountains which represent goals at times and barriers at other times. I'm grateful to God that Chris's mountains, with the valleys and crevices as well, led her to the very heights! Tom requested that "For me to live is Christ and to die is gain" be etched on the white marble slab with the bronze cross that marked his wife's grave.

Sotira, the Greek Bible woman, hugged me when Bill and I were ready to leave Athens, exhorting, "God has a period on the matter here. Don't leave it with a questions mark." I had performed the task of auditing books, investigating personnel, dismissing employees, closing accounts, selling properties and giving thorough reports to the Headquarters office. I had done what I was supposed to do. A friend reassured me, "Success is not what you have done compared to what others have done, but what you have done compared to what you were supposed to do. To be successful is to finish the originally intended assignment according to the plan and the specifications of your Creator. You completed your assignment. Therefore you've been successful."

## 94 I HAD TO SING! (1991)

*"The Lord hath been mindful of us:...He will bless them that fear the Lord,"* Psalm 115:12-13. I read that declaration of faith from the psalmist when I left the Cardiac Family Waiting Room to walk around the eight blocks surrounding the hospital in Indianapolis, singing all the way! The surgeon informed me that Bill's complications were over and we could expect a normal recovery after encountering so many problems, including a mild stroke. It was time to sing. Oh, some people looked curiously at me, but I didn't care. I just had to sing to the Lord! My Bill was going to recover well. Hallelujah!

Toward the end of 1990, we came to the U.S. from Greece to minister in some churches, visiting prayer partners and donors. We got to spend Christmas with our son and his family as well. Bill had been experiencing angina since 1975, but he never made a big issue of it. That's the way he is! Upon returning to Greenwood he had a heart catheterization which was complicated by many minutes of hemorrhaging. The following Monday, the angioplasty procedure was not successful. Again he hemorrhaged. His heart stopped. I was scared! Our son came to encourage us and to give me a strong shoulder to lean on. February 21st, very early on a Thursday morning, we three sang in harmony as the nurses rolled Bill down the corridor. The surgery included a coronary artery bypass which included three vessels of the left side of the heart along with a replacement of the aortic valve. The surgery was over six hours long. Our son and I talked about the brilliant creativity our merciful God has given to the medical profession.

During those days in the Family Waiting Room, our son Bill, and I were able to minister to distraught wives and worried family members.

I have a sweet picture in my memory of Bill kneeling before a weeping woman, taking her hands and praying God's peace for her. Then he secured a card table and purchased a puzzle for a lonely wife who had to wait a long time for word about her husband. We even sang God's comfort for them.

The medical expense was going to be immense! The OMS office notified our mailing list partners of the need. An anonymous gift of $10,000 surprised me. A church in Cuenca, Ecuador sent a check for $1,000, which brought sobs of humility to me. One church in Spain sent $300 and another sent $200. All that added up to an awareness of God's loving care and ample supply. The Lord is indeed mindful of His own. Phyllis Erny, one of our OMS co-workers, planted an idea that sprouted into a reality to request that the hospital give us a reduction in the charges. We prepared the way with prayer. When I entered the head cashier's office, she extended her hand with a smile to say, "Oh, I remember you. When your husband was discharged I said to myself, 'I'd like to know that couple. That woman's smile tells me she's different.' And now you're here!"

God gave me favor with her. The Holy Spirit opened an hour of dialogue as she shared some very intricate involvements that reminded me of a soap opera. After crying with her and praying for her, I inquired about our bill. She even approached the cardiologists' group on our behalf. They gave us some discount as well because of our low-income status. She worked on lessening the hospital charges. God really made the crooked places straight.

I kept on singing—through the hernia repair and bladder and prostate surgery later. Eventually, we faced atrial fibrillation and a staph infection in the chest as well as the installation of a dual demand pacemaker which could not prevent the congestive heart failure that plagued him after that. In his later years, God gave me the strength to keep him in our home as his caretaker while Alzheimer's disease stole away his wonderful mental prowess although it never touched his sweet and loving character nor his ability to pray beautifully and thoughtfully for others.

## 95 THE FIRE PROVED WE WERE A GOOD TEAM (1993)

When Bill completely recovered from his heart surgeries along with other necessary medical interventions in Indiana, God returned us to the Iberian Peninsula. I offered to step in to fill the gap at the Rock of Horeb Camp. John Vimont, well-trained in camp management, was off the field as were others who had previously helped to run the camp. Therefore, I became responsible for administration, accounting, personnel supervision, and on several occasions, management of the kitchen while Bill concentrated on evangelism in the nearby villages.

Our team members differed in very interesting ways. At times, I returned to our little cottage on the hill, not knowing whether to laugh or cry. People vary in so many ways, the time of day they function best, the habitual speed of working, their sense of humor or lack of it, their taste in clothing and music. One work problem was resolved by agreeing that one person worked best in the afternoon and evening while the other one worked best in the early morning. I learned it was not so important WHEN their jobs were done, but rather, that the results were good, so long as work habits didn't conflict with our service to the people who came to the camp. Except for the kitchen, dining room and some services to the campers, schedules were changed to make team members happy, each one working at his or her own speed, in the best productive hours of that person's day. Before that arrangement had been made, faster people drove slower colleagues beyond their strength while slower ones held the faster ones back to the point of screaming frustration.

We had summer workers from the British Isles and the U.S.A. along with volunteers from Madrid churches. Camps were continuous. Rosalia, the camp housekeeper who was my "right hand girl" made sure the dormitories glisten after each group left the premises.

One week's group brought over 700 ex-alcoholics and ex-drug addicts with their counselors and teachers to the camp. Our dorms couldn't hold them all, so tents dotted the surrounding fields. Over one hundred people were baptized in the river or in the swimming pool. Up and down, up and down, up and down. How many times did I sprint up and down the path to the dining hall? How many mounds of potatoes were peeled? How many meatballs did I fry? How many pots of soup did the cook prepare? I can't remember nor do I even WANT to remember! If you could only have seen the mountains of garbage from such a large group! That alone was a small organizational matter to resolve.

I made three decisions upon arrival at the camp. 1. We would use things from the shop/repair garage before spending money for new stuff. 2. We would invite two or even three small groups to share the camp facilities simultaneously which would help diminish the debt. 3. A thorough inventory would be made, including examination of the existing fire extinguishers. Some of the volunteers groaned but everyone cooperated. The inventory list was typed and filed. We all went about the daily business of running a busy campground until one day I heard Xavier holler, "Hey! Isn't that smoke coming from the repair shop?"

He grabbed the extinguisher from the kitchen. Rosalia raced to the dorm for another extinguisher, Ben to another building for the other one. Everyone ran "lickety-split" down the hill to the shop. By that time, the volunteer down there had begun to use the extinguisher from the shop. The capricious flames were hard to put out but the marvelous tem work performed the feat of extinguishing the remorseless flames. I called the insurance company after informing Scott Murphy, our field director in Madrid. With grimy smudges on our sweaty faces, we all gathered in the kitchen, our sighs mingled with expressions of gratitude, "Thank the Lord—nobody's hurt."

It was hard to quell my nervousness the next afternoon when the insurance inspector arrived. He took photographs, looked around, smiled and said, "Could I have that cup of coffee you offered me?" As he sipped he looked over the list our maintenance fellows had prepared for me of those things that had been destroyed or damaged. Beside each item I had typed the cost of complete repair or replacement. Clipped to that list was our recent complete inventory. "Well, well," the inspector said. "This is very impressive. This is what I will do. I'll leave a check with you today. Keep a receipt of everything you purchase for repair or replacement. Let me know when you go beyond $300.00 and I'll see that you get all you need." I don't think he really perceived how flabbergasted I felt! Bill then took over the conversation. Never one to miss an opportunity to share the gospel with anyone he came into contact, he led him to at least acknowledge that he did not know Christ personally. He then told him how he could be ready for heaven.

That year I presented the following statistic to the Annual Field Meeting:

> 58 different camps, retreats or seminars at Rock of Horeb
>
> 3,395 campers
>
> 22 public professions of faith in Christ
>
> 30 rededications, including a call to ministry
>
> 260 baptisms

Whenever I walked from our cottage to the office, meandering through the little forest to the Casa Grande (Big House) or went up to the dining room to welcome a new group, I was reminded on every side of the helpful hands of the men and women of Men for Missions, both from Great Britain and North America, who came to build, repair, and install, whatever was needed. One man from Devon, England gave us such excellent advice on sewers and septic tanks we saved almost a thousand dollars!

Toward the end of our time there, I could report that we were completely out of debt. All heaters, all toilets, all kitchen machines were in working order. I wish the same could be said of me! One afternoon, I prepared a pot of soup to take to the cook who was not feeling well. I had already changed into my sleep clothes for it was the "free day" between camps. On my return to our cottage, I fell down about nine yards of stone steps, breaking my front teeth and bruising my arthritic body badly. I was glad to lie in bed for a couple of days. What a way to end our assignment at the camp!

# 96 SHE TURNED HER BACK ON GOD (1993)

Ximena came to the Rock of Horeb camp to serve as a volunteer. I'm grateful that God gives me opportunities not only to listen to people and pray with them but also to appreciate God's dealings with them. One day Ximena and I sat under the pine trees chatting about the changes God makes in our lives. She told me her story.

> "My family was traditionally Roman Catholic, but did not devoutly practice their religion. I always heard about God as a powerful, distant and good Being but one to be afraid of. I often prayed to Him when I was a little girl, but I started to doubt His existence because my petitions were not granted. I didn't know God personally. I wanted Him to do MY WILL! I was really unsettled and unhappy when my parents separated when I was twelve years old. Since God didn't prevent that I became very angry with Him. My sister and I went to live with my father in Chile, far away from family and friends. I began a different life in a new school with new friends in a strange, difficult place. God seemed farther and farther away.
>
> At fifteen years of age, people called me a "rebel". I loved wild parties, lots of joking friends, alcohol, new adventures, etc. My father was always trying to control my life and that made me rebel even more. My stubbornness went beyond all authority and punishment. If Dad punished me by ordering me to remain in the house I sneaked out through the window and disappeared for a few days. Finally, my family and Dad gave up on me. I was free! I thought that was overwhelmingly wonderful!

I was seventeen years old when I left home, feeling very independent. I studied photography. I joined the "punk" crowd. All my tastes, my opinions, and my morals were different from what some people considered normal. I called myself an atheist. The most important things were myself and my art. I involved myself in all areas of artistic environment—theater, cinema, photography and painting, which implied that I worked in each of them, relating to unusual people with both good and bad morals. I moved in with my boyfriend, an artist with whom I worked. He was my friend and my companion in fun. We did absolutely everything together.

Then, for some reason, I began to wonder about my life. I started to think that I was probably a bad girl. Yet, I still stubbornly rejected that thought when it invaded my awareness. I was fighting within myself. I felt ashamed when I realized that God was talking to my heart. I went on like that for about a year, trying to deny it all. But God was there nonetheless, clearly calling again and again at my heart's door even though I was turning my back on Him.

I started to read the Bible and discuss it with my lover. Together, we began to recognize that God was everywhere, even there with us. We prayed at times, but made no effort to change our lifestyle.

My love, Alvaro, made plans for us to travel around the world to visit exotic places and to get acquainted with other artists of different cultures. On my own, I was praying more, trying to find God. Since then, many things have happened for which I have no explanation, things that only God could have arranged to bring me to this point.

As we traveled, I vacillated in my urge to look for God. Upon arriving in Spain, I rang the operator requesting the phone number of an evangelical church. She gave me the address and phone number of the OMS church in Moratalaz, a neighborhood of Madrid. The people were lovingly attentive to me. I remembered then that my grandmother had taken me to a Gospel church twice when I lived with her briefly and I remember sensing that God was there in that church. God was breaking me more and more as I continued going to the Moratalaz church. He began to win!

I finally yielded and accepted Jesus as my personal Savior. I wanted more and more of His love. But I had to decide that I was really going to obey the Lord. I had to let Him change my lifestyle. It would mean I had to leave the man I loved, my best friend, and the only link with my art. And I would probably have to leave my job in the theater. By that time, I had stopped using drugs, but it was very obvious that in my own strength, I could NOT break away from my lifestyle. It seemed so crazy! I was leaving everything! My heart was hurting, so I separated myself from the church. I TURNED MY BACK ON GOD."

Ximena leaned on my shoulder, emotionally remembering those days behind her. "Then what happened that you got here?" I asked. "After a few months I admitted to God that I had no peace. So I begged for His help. I was not able to even imagine what my future could be. I knew I'd have to step out into thin air. Only God would fill the ground beneath my feet. I had to choose, Alvaro or Christ."

"I understand, Ximena," I said as I handed her a handkerchief to wipe away her tears.

"God miraculously answered. He showed me that very same day a plan for me for the summer. He gave me a spiritual family, a loving sister in the Lord, Laura Duran, the pastor's wife. She showed me how God would fill my life with joy and soothe my broken heart."

Ximena and I hugged each other and prayed together, thanking God that she had joined the volunteers at the camp. After her discipleship classes with the pastor's wife, Ximena was ready for the daily discipline, hard work, and the interpersonal relationship with Christ at the camp.

# RETIREMENT TO FLORIDA

Abe Lincoln said, "I walk slowly, but I never walk backwards."

## 97 I ALWAYS SEND BILL OFF WITH A PRAYER AND A KISS (1997)

God gave us a lovely little house in the Bradenton Missionary Village, in Bradenton, Florida, provided by a dedicated entrepreneur, Anthony Rossi, who established TROPICANA (citrus juices). Every Thursday at noon Bill and I would stand in the living room, our hands clasped in prayer, as I commended him into the control of the Holy Spirit. Since 1994, he has been involved in a one on one ministry of witness and encouragement in the County Jail each week. The men, most of them murderers or repeated rapists, are waiting for final sentencing. No assembly time is permitted so Bill and the other volunteers cannot have an evangelistic service of any kind. This has not perturbed Bill for one of his greatest gifts is witnessing and counseling, giving loving personal attention. About seventy-five percent of the men have not had a father figure as mentor and advisor. Bill, with his loving attitude, his almost white beard, and his years of experience, serves them as "papa".

While I was in the hospital, recuperating from total left knee replacement surgery, I cried often because the therapy was horribly unpleasant. One day, however, I cried tears of joy and gratitude when I read a letter addressed to me from Joseph, one of the inmates of the County Jail:

> *I am one of Mr. Miller's students and his friend. My wife and I have been charged with the murder of our son. My letter is not to tell you about us, but rather to tell you what a beautiful man your dear, pure-minded husband is. What a blessing to the boys in 'H Pod'. God shows He truly loves us because He sent us Mr. Miller. When we're in despair, overwhelmed with anxiety and our imagina-*

> *tions are raging, and when our hope almost diminishes, the Lord fills Mr. Miller with the Holy Spirit and sends him here to us, to encourage and pray with us. He has literally told us that peace beyond understanding is free and available through Jesus who never fails. Mrs. Miller, I have wanted to tell you how very much Mr. Miller is loved by each one of us. Today, we had an opportunity to return the love he has taught us to have. He told us about your recent surgery and the pain and discomfort you experience. It was very clear to us that he has been shaken by this. His love for you is very obvious. The Holy Spirit led us to ask Mr. Miller to have a seat, so we could make a circle around him, lay our hands on him, and pray for him and for YOU, for God to heal you quickly. Praise God that we four believers could serve God this way.*

I have always sent Bill off on Thursdays with prayer and a resounding kiss. The spiritual battle is real but we know that the Lord is Victor!

## 98  "I HATE YOU, I HATE YOU!" (1997)

We returned to Spain for a short ministry tour. I stood on the steps of the Motril church watching Manuel as he hurried toward us. Even before he got close enough to clasp my hand, I saw the tears in his eyes. With a flash of memory, I went back to a day in 1982.

The house was full of people. I was talking to guests, getting lunch, directing my pre-teen cleaning girl on how to scrub a bathroom, encouraging little Sarah to be satisfied with the coloring materials I had put out for her, when the doorbell rang. I thought to myself, "I hope it is just Bill who forgot his key." Instead, there stood Manuel, my neighbor's husband, drunk and livid with rage. He stormed at me, "I want you and your husband to know that God does NOT exist. Jesus Christ is NOT alive and there is no such thing as love."

I couldn't move. He went on to explain with a horrible expression on his red face that cut straight through to my heart. He was miserable in his sin and rejection and did not want to admit any need. He had failed many times in jobs and other endeavors. He needed our love but rejected it at the same time. He didn't want to accept anyone else's love either. The church congregation paid his wife's electric bill when he left home. He never expressed any thanks. He never acknowledged the gifts of clothing and food for his wife and four daughters. It must have been very hard for him to face the fact that he did not provide for his family.

Flashes of memory are lightning quick. Then I remembered how Manuel told us that he had us investigated because he was sure we were C.I.A. agents. When he said that, Bill and I chuckled and I said, "Oh, Manuel, you weren't the first to do that. The husband of one of the women in the Bible study in Madrid did the same thing. He was even mad when he found out it wasn't true! He said 'How can those people live on what they receive each month! They're poor!' So now you know."

Rosa, his wife, told me that she was almost sure that he was responsible for the three times we had returned to our apartment after church services to find the kitchen drawers emptied out on the floor and our files strewn all over. Nothing was ever stolen, just messes made to cause our frustration. And now, standing before me, erect and dressed in a suit and tie, was that man who declared that he hated us!

His big arms enfolded us both and his voice broke as he said, "Dear brother and sister, please forgive me for all the evil speaking and hateful things I did. I now belong to the Lord and I'm very sorry I was so slow to come to Him. Can you pardon me? Will you forgive me? I want to have peace in my heart."

Manuel no longer was his family's phrase for him, "the angry, lazy man of hate" but a man of prayer responsible for the intercessory groups in the church. He had passed through deep waters of physical pain and weakness, but now God, whose way is perfect, had changed his hate to love. I didn't count the times he said, "I love you dear ones," while we were in his home, in his church, and walking with him in the park.

# 99  A MURDERER SLEPT IN OUR GUEST ROOM! (1998)

Shortly after we arrived in Ecuador, Bill was transmitting on the short wave radio set in January of 1956. He had received the message that the five missionary men who had gone to the jungle to make contact with the Auca Indians, had been speared to death by Indians on the beach of the Curaray River. You may have read about it in Elisabeth Elliot's books or seen a video about the incident. That incident was part of our orientation to Ecuador and God made a deep impression on our hearts because of it.

In February of 1998, Bill and I offered to extend hospitality to the two Indians who were accompanying Jesse Saint, grandson of Nate, the missionary pilot of the evangelism project to the Aucas. Steve, Nate's son, was with them, too.

Bill and I hurried home from the evening church service that Sunday and waited, excited with anticipation. The four arrived about eight thirty in the evening. How affectionate the Indians were in their greeting! When we sat down on the sofa Steve informed us immediately that "Auca" really means "naked savage". He informed us, "It is degrading to say 'Auca'. That's the name the whites in Ecuador gave to the Indian tribe. We should refer to them as the 'Wuarani'. They call themselves 'the people'. Until the Gospel made its impact, they always referred to the 'other people' who were not Wuarani as the 'half-humans'.

Tementa is the son of Nikomi, one of those who killed the missionaries. Nikomi went to the Evangelism Congress in Berlin with Rachel Saint. He was full of information when he returned to his people. As a result,

Tementa was mentally prepared for the culture shock of the U.S. Mincaiya, in spite of being approximately sixty-eight years old (he's not really sure of his exact age), just accepted everything as part of the different U.S. world, but he was often amused. Both were fascinated with faucets and toilets. They said through translation, "So many ways to make the water run (or flush)." They were fascinated with hot water coming from the pipes. They took two showers a day if they could. It was not because of being dirty or sweaty, simply for its novelty!

Steve told of their first visit to the supermarket. Mincaiya beamed from ear to ear, looked all around him and declared, "If I lived in the U.S. I'd live in THIS house. I would never go hungry." His statement reminded me that the Indians eat only when there is food available from hunting. When there is no food, they just don't eat for a while! They said with a laugh, "We sure like the eating schedule here. Morning, noon, late afternoon and sometimes in the evening everybody eats."

Mincaiya doesn't speak English except for a couple of phrases he's picked up from Jesse. While they were in that supermarket, the men were wearing their headdresses because they had just come from a special missionary meeting. An older woman came up to Steve in the aisle and whispered, "They aren't from around here, are they? They probably don't speak any English, right?"

"No, they don't." Steve answered.

In that very moment, Mincaiya beamed at the woman and said, "Hi!" She jumped and scurried away.

Another thing that impressed them was the straight roads on our highways. The jungle, as you can imagine, usually has no roads, only paths, and those are rarely straight lines.

I found it amusing that for a place where time and schedules have no significance, they purchased watches as gifts for their wives!

I took them to the kitchen. It was after nine o'clock so Jesse said, "Just a little snack will be O.K." I gave them baked sweet potatoes, big rolls, honey, cheese and bananas. They ate as though they hadn't had a meal for two days although only two hours earlier they had stopped at Wendy's with Jesse for hamburgers.

Their testimonies produced tears of joy to our eyes. Mincaiya said, "Before Jesus my heart was very dark and I was full of hate. Now I love because the Light of Jesus fills my heart."

Tementa told us, "We are elders in our churches. More than ten percent of our settlement is now Christian." Steve told us that North Americans and Europeans have visited what they call "Aucaland" and that although most have been prudent in giving statistical information, others either have not had the integrity or heard only what they wanted to hear or seen only what they wanted to see. Therefore, what they reported was colored by their warped perspective and interpretation. Some have even reported in error here in the States that eighty-five percent of the Indians are baptized Christians!

The men were visibly moved when they talked about being aware that God's people are all over the world. We prayed together in three languages—English, Spanish, and Wuarani. Tementa took the initiative to pray for us retired missionaries in this village, thanking the Lord for our dedication and perseverance. That brought more tears! Then Mincaiya prayed that we would be well protected, never have an empty stomach, and that we would keep on telling other people about God.

When they left after lunch on Monday, I was still on a "spiritual high" so keyed up that I couldn't get down to any mundane task! I thought about Steve's parting words, "A fellow in Timbuktu gave his life for full-time service as a result of that incident on the Curaray River. Chuck Swindoll, noted author, made his dedication as a result of reading about "the martyrs". When our young people of the Madrid Tabernacle gave a dramatic reading at the Women's Retreat in El Escorial about the "martyrs of Curaray" a lay-priest had a born-again experience which then led him to go to work among the lepers of Africa. Only eternity will reveal what was done for God's glory by the laying down of those five lives.

On Monday, we said our farewell words to Mincaiya who is known affectionately as Grandpa and whose ear lobes hung down with big holes where he had previously inserted bamboo pieces. Mincaiyas smile was charmingly infectious and he was not embarrassed to hold a brother's hand or to pat young Jesse on the back. We said goodbye to Tementa who served as the interpreter-informant for Rachel Saint and then for K. Pike with the result that now the Indians have part of the New Testament in their language. This then required that schools be established since no one knew what a book was or what to do with it!

Wow! The indelible impact of that past murderer and the son of a past murderer quickened our spirits and revived our burden to persevere in intercession for the lost. When they left, my heart sang out, "Praise the Lord, oh, yes, praise the Lord!"

## 100 SHE STOLE AWAY TO JESUS (1989)

Jean blinked her eyes and the nurse's aid gasped in surprise. I had just finished singing *His Eye Is on the Sparrow* beside her bed. I continued stroking her arm, murmuring, "Jesus loves you so much, Jean. Remember how you asked Him to forgive your sins and you acknowledged His as your personal Lord and Savior?" There was no movement, not even a wiggle of her little finger. But she blinked her eyes in response.

Several months previous to my bedside song I had gone to the Convalescent Home to give a mini-concert. As the wheelchairs were pushed into the room, I greeted the patients. I noticed the well-dressed, white-haired woman endeavoring to sit erect. Her scowl caught my eye. She declared to me, "I'm here only because they told me you know how to sing. Mind you, I know my music. For many years, I played flute in the Boston Symphony. Oh, and I want you to know that I'm an atheist. God does not interest me."

When I returned to sing a few weeks later that same woman, Jean McCormick, sat next to the exit door. However, in coming for the music, she could not escape my words of personal testimony. A team of women from the Missionary Village where we live visited the patients each week. They too, were faithful to minister to Jean. Our prayer partners were praying for her. I wasn't convinced of her atheistic stance. I turned out to be right—it was a mask to hold on to her private nature. It was the Holy Spirit who got through to her heart. Several weeks after her profession of faith, she went into a coma. One day as I prayed for Jean, I was gently impressed to visit her. "But why?" my colleague asked.

I replied, "When I was in the last hours of coma in the throes of tetanus many years ago, I heard the missionary nurse reading from the book of Hebrews. I couldn't move a toe, but I was aware of her voice. Maybe the Lord will use my song to bless Jean."

After Jean blinked her eyes, I sang *Amazing Grace* with all my heart. As I finished the phrase, "We've no less days to sing God's praise than when we've first begun." I saw her lips move. I leaned down and heard a quaking whisper, "It's true."

Her lips shut. Not a movement. Not a sign of life. I sang "Steal Away to Jesus" and said, "Jean, I'm so glad you're ready to go when He calls you." The nurse's aid was speechless. I instructed her to tune Jean's radio to the classical music station or to the Christian station in the early morning and late night when they aired the traditional hymns.

Our prayer partners and I were happy when our new sister in Christ slipped away to Jesus a few weeks later. From this experience I want to encourage Christians to pray earnestly, even for the conversion of "atheists" and also, to obey the impression to read or sing for those who may seem "far away". We can help them on their journey to "steal away to Jesus!"

# EPILOGUE
## By Darlene Miller

Lois Jean Pankuch Miller has now "stolen away" to her precious Jesus. She sang and quoted comforting words of Scripture as she awaited what was supposed to be a simple procedure going through her rib to repair a bad valve in her heart. She sang and quoted Bible verses down the hospital halls on her gurney all the way to surgery. How she yearned to have some more time to do more for the Lord. She was so grateful to the Lord for loving her that she felt she could not do enough in a lifetime. We reminded her that He loved her just for herself, too. Yet, not being able to keep up with her singing, writing, performing her monologues, teaching or speaking was a trial for her. Until her health failed her, discipline and sense of purpose meant she used every opportunity to be purposeful in her endeavors always striving to do it well, in fact, with excellence. Someone wrote in a card after her death that our Mom showed people how to keep going on despite pain and infirmity.

In my mind's eye I see her waiting for us immaculately dressed with matching accessories and her hair neatly, stylishly in place. She adapted the time it took to prepare herself and her home for hospitality. She simplified the varied international dishes she served but she persevered never dwindling in her desire to extend herself to others in her ministry of teaching, music and personal encouragement, always with a certain flare. Truly, people had no idea how badly or how weak she felt at times. Her spirit carried her.

On her desk was her latest writing project, beside her chair materials to study in preparation for a class. Music was nearby to review for the next expected involvement or envisioned possibility. Notebooks to jot ideas as they came, her calendar carefully annotated for birthdays and events.

Retyping and editing this book brought me closer than ever to my "suegra" (mother-in-law) whom I deeply loved and admired. As I typed, I pictured her in each of these ventures, or better yet, adventures. Her clear, beautiful singing voice is captured in treasured moments by our family and by so many around the world. Her spectacular hospitality with her gifts for creating beauty in her surroundings as well as her culinary skills will be equally remembered. Her creativity, whether in problem solving, writing or planning events like the live nativity at her church was almost legendary. She had a way of making mundane things special like putting together fun, spontaneous picnics. She had a special way with children. They listened to her, obeying her readily to everyone's amazement.

She was an extraordinary woman.

When we were in Ecuador, we were struck with the respect with which both Mom and Dad were held. One pastor of a large church in Ecuador whom Mom taught piano and mentored for many years said, "It was not what they taught, although that was a wonderful thing. It was how they LIVED, what they taught in everyday life faithfully that made them so precious to us." They modeled the Christian walk. They were the Word in Action.

When I returned and relayed to a tearful Mom all I heard and experienced I told her, "Mom, if any one person would say such admirable things about me when my work is done, I would be happy." She never missed an opportunity to give God the glory.

Mom did not survive the "simple" surgery. Staph infections had deteriorated the tissue of her heart making it impossible to attach the new valve or to stop the bleeding that resulted by trying to stitch it into the damaged organ. She slipped away peacefully never regaining consciousness while still in the operating room. We thanked God that we were there with her as well as several friends from 'Bradenton Missionary Village' and her faithful pastor, Rev. Dr. Thurl Mann. They sustained us with their presence and prayers. Within two weeks, two of her closest friends followed her "home". I comforted myself picturing these precious women being told by the Savior they loved and served, "Well, done, thou good and faithful servant." I also pictured the joyous reunion for three elderly, ailing women as they celebrated their new bodies with a lovely tea-time, sharing the stories that have enthralled us here.

As we prepare to go to Ecuador ourselves to minister to some of those who became God's servants in response to the call of God through the Word delivered by Mom and Dad and their team members, we are inspired with a sense of the sacred. Our generation, enjoying the fruit and a wealth of varied roles in the Church of Jesus Christ, continues the work on a foundation built with the blood of the martyrs, others who answered God's call and who lived through the difficulties with a grace only God's Spirit can give. Mom and Dad Miller served faithfully wherever they were called which included, 19 years in Ecuador, 2 in Greece and 20 years in their beloved Spain. It is indeed humbling and energizing to think that it is truly God who goes before us, calling us to the ventures, or better said, adventures to which He calls us. This little collection of vignettes gives a flavor of the life of a missionary. We pray that you have been blessed to consider how God uses imperfect, ordinary but surrendered vessels to His glory. May you be prompted to pray all the more for those who answer the Lord's call realizing as these stories have demonstrated that it creates an essential partnership. Those who go could not do what they do without the support in finances and prayer that make it possible.

I prepare this for publication with a heart overflowing with gratitude for having had the opportunity for inspiring conversation, prayer fellowship, and leisurely dinners which expanded my perspectives and increased my appreciation for this delightful lady with the sparkling eyes. I felt honored to be included in her battles and celebrations. Of course, we can't forget the fun and humorous moments either. Soon after helping bathe her in a rehab facility she said with a twinkle, "You can go now, I've seen enough of you and you've definitely seen enough of me!" Our last visit ended in one of those sweet holy benedictions that linger as you walk the corridors of time, "Nos vemos en el cielo, mi Mámi ¡querida!" (My dearest Mom, See you in heaven!)

# A POSTSCRIPT FROM A GRATEFUL SON

The cycle of human life as God designed us ushers in a review of meaning for our life with greater persistence as we approach the end of our life. This yearning to know transcendence and the legacy we may leave to a succeeding generation was evidenced in my Dad's ponderings even as his body began robbing him of the ability to intellectually investigate and integrate his varied life experiences. His petitions in prayer, his voiced disjointed memories, and his comments along the way were an awakening process for my Mom as she continued to enjoy expressing her lessons learned in life in literary, artistic, and musical ways. Her visiting concerns about her aging voice could not stifle her singing over the morning birds as she awoke. "Por la mañana yo dirijo mi alabanza, al Dios que ha sido y es mi única esperanza…" (In the morning I lift my praise to God who is my only hope!) She was compelled to use her lung-power in congregational worship, "Then sings my soul…", nor could my Mom resist interjecting song phrases in dinner conversation, nighttime prayers, or telephone exhortations. My Mom certainly benefited from the integration of life reviews, but without skipping a heartbeat expending energies focused on the needs of others and on the opportunities the Holy Spirit gave her to declare the awesome deeds of the One who had "called her out of darkness into His marvelous light!"

As Mom recaptured a significant portion of her life in "Stretched but not Broken", she offers a portrait of missionary life in true poignant stories, real life of real people. Recent reading transported me to the anxiety of reading Scripture to "Frenchie". How my childlike heart prayed aching for her soul to be touched! The vignettes repeatedly flashed for me moments of listening to people, wrestling with their fears, their addictions, or bitterness while in counsel with Mom or even during a meal at our table. I vividly recall the slaps across my face in "Boca de los Sapos" by an angered passerby who threw my offered 'tract' by the wayside. And I smile as I think of great events shared with traveling, visiting musicians who shared in open air meetings, parks, churches, and theaters giving testimony to a loving, satisfying, healing, personal Savior, Jesus!

My parents openly modeled for me honest-to-goodness piety without pretension and with songs or shouts of excitement when God's Grace and Mercy brought transformation to the nitty-gritty reality of anyone around us. The authentic comforting of a God who incarnationally identifies with us and sends His Spirit in personalized tailored ministry stared at me in the face as I watched my parents lives. Many of these stories I have heard repeatedly in the homes of dear people who gave of themselves in warm affectionate hospitality during deputation, also in Camp Meetings and Missionary Conventions, as well as in our own living room. At times I thought my Mom was a tad melodramatic (OK…quite dramatic, Latin style!) as she seemed to have a special way of accentuating the point of her story. Through it all, the desire for God's Glory to shine came through.

Truly, missionaries are regular people who have responded to the Call of God. Of course missionaries are at their best when they are diligent to pursue after God and are sensitive to His direction, delighting to do His will (Prov. 15:9; Prov. 3:5-7; Prov. 1:23), when they allow the discipline of the Lord to bring them to humility and renewal (Ps. 51:7-13; Heb. 12:1-13), and when they hunger more and more for the infilling of God's Spirit (Matthew 5:6; Ephesians 5:15-20). Then, they are willing to take risks in faith, ready to serve despite inconveniences, and become adaptable to almost any situation as they long to honor the Lord with an attitude that draws people to Jesus as well as by convincing words and actions.

That being said, all whom the Lord has graciously saved and called, He seeks to empower and direct. This includes all of us disciples, believers just now taking baby steps, deacons who are butchers or builders during the week, teachers and lawyers, congressmen, and community developers, and yes, a devoted missionary. Mom who was persistent to pray for her son, always speaking the truth in love, affirming obedience, and letting him see her being stretched, being made in the image of the One who shed His precious blood for the whole world.

May we be moved by the Holy Spirit of God and follow the honored path of missionary servants in the roles and callings that the Lord of the Church gives us. Worthy is the Lamb to receive all honor and glory, Amen!

Printed in the United States
136442LV00001B/4/P